Mary "tl

MW00878896

Sue Anna Hunt

To: Ann Marie

MAY THE LORD
BLESS YOU AND KEEP YOU

Sue a. Hunt

Eph. 3:20

1

Mary *"the"* Last

Sue Anna Hunt

Copyright © Sue Anna Hunt 2017

The conversations in the book all come from the author's recollections, though they are not written to represent word-for-word transcripts. Rather, the author has retold them in a way that evokes the feeling and meaning what was said and in all instances, the essence of the dialogue is accurate.

ACKNOWLEDGMENTS

Special thanks to all who helped my dream become a reality—

- Members of the Val McGee Writing Forum,
- Authors Helen Taylor Andrews and Cheri Blackmon along with Alyssa whose help was indispensable,
- My friends who've patiently waited for me to finish this book, and
- To my family who I pray will carry my legacy of faith to generations to come.

In loving memory of my late husband, Willard, who encouraged me to pursue my goal with diligence.

Table of Contents

INTRODUCTION

It is Monday, June 27, 2016 at 6:58 AM.

Today is a very important day in my life. I am going to start a task I have wanted to do for more than twenty years. I am going to write a book and it's all about me. Yes, me! I know how this must sound to you. You must be asking, as I have asked myself time and time again, what's special about me. The answer…nothing. And that is why I must write my story. Dr. R. Joseph, a neuroscientist, said, "Within the core of each child constitutes the foundation of what we have become, who we are, and what we will be."

I want you, the reader, to grasp a complete understanding of what this particular child has experienced so far. But it's not only about me. That's what I hope will stimulate your interest in my story. This account will include others…some others…many others… known and unknown others, who have been involved thus far in my nearly 84 years on this earth. Others who have reared me, taught me, and challenged me to become the person I've become this day. However, most is still all about me and my choices--some good, some selfish, some destructive, and many life-changing ones.

My story will be told in a somewhat different format than that which is familiar to the accomplished reader, but sojourn with me. I am going to take you on an excursion through my life using a variation of facts experienced not only by me, but by those others who were mentioned earlier.

The method I will implement is that of short tales intertwined with narratives. These "talk stories" will be used as fillers. I was introduced to this concept of writing when my oldest daughter, Deborah, was attending Spalding University in Louisville, Kentucky. She was assigned a book to read entitled *The Warrior Woman* by Maxine Hong Kingston. Subsequently, she asked me to write about some events from my life along with those tales that have been passed down through our family. After completing writing four or five incidents worth retelling, I saw the value of using this form to preserve a small part of my past for my children and grandchildren. It is my hope that this format will make reading my story more enjoyable.

An even more perplexing question for me as I begin to write is-- where do I begin? The answer is obvious. I will begin the saga of me at the beginning of me. As stated in *A&E Biography:* "Every life has a story." I would like to introduce "Mary *the* Last" to you…Me.

PART I

CHILDHOOD

*"Life can only be understood backwards, but it must be lived forwards." (*Soren Kierkegaard)

A loud scream rang through the countryside of a small rural community of Bloomfield, Kentucky. It was a sound mixed with pain, joy, and anticipation coming from a woman delivering a child. But it wasn't just any child, it was me… making my grand entrance at 4 a.m. on what must have been a hot day in August 6, 1932. There, waiting to welcome me along with the country doctor, was my father, Robert Lee Guthrie and, of course, my mother, Cordie Mae Simpson Guthrie.

What a welcoming committee! I could feel it! This is going to be an exciting life!

Some helpful tidbits about my parents would probably be welcomed at this point. So, tarry with me a bit while I give you a short, but incomplete genealogy.

My mother was a very young widow of 34 years and who had six other children ranging in age from 3 ½ to 19 years when I was born. Their last name was Foster. My father was an elderly widower who had eight adult children born to the Guthrie clan. At the time of my birth, the youngest Guthrie child was 20 years old, while the oldest was approximately 45-50 years of age. So, one can foresee some of the drama that might possibly occur when a baby was put into the mix.

Dr. Hetihitt asked, "Well Cordie, it's a girl! What do you want to name her?"

And that's where to story of me really begins. Let me share it with you through this *Talk Story.*

DISCOVERING MY "REAL" NAME

When I was 17 years of age, I learned that the name everyone had called me all of my life was not the one that was on the official document of the state of Kentucky. What a shocker! It happened like this.

I graduated Central High School in June, 1950 and soon afterwards applied for summer employment at Enro Shirt Company in Louisville. One of the stipulations required for me to begin work was that I had to secure a copy of my birth certificate, since I was under the age of eighteen. You might note that this happened before the emergence of the many of the electronic devices we have today. However, I didn't perceive a problem getting my birth record forthright. So, I went downtown to the Department of Vital Statistics to obtain an application.

After waiting patiently for weeks upon weeks, I finally got the call I'd been waiting for. I now could begin working and saving for Business School. Excitedly, I entered the office with the $2 fee in hand. The clerk showed me my birth certificate and began to explain why it took so long for them to receive it. She only had to show me the top line and there it was! First name, Mary; middle name, "the", and last name, Last. They couldn't explain it. I couldn't explain it, but I knew somebody who could…Mama.

I took the certificate and hurried home for an explanation. After all, I had been called Sue Anna Guthrie all this time and none of these names were on that certified copy. I showed it to my mother with confusion pasted plainly on my face. Mama looked at the certificate and when she saw what had been done, she burst out laughing. Of course, I didn't see anything funny about it at all.

Mama explained that when she and my father got married, she had sighed a big relief at the thought of not having any more children. She was only 35 years old when I was born, but Dad was (according to her) way up in age. Our family bible recorded his age as 58. I guess she thought he was too old to have more children and then, "surprise", here I come. She went on to explain that I was born at home so the family doctor dutifully delivered me. Mama went on to say that after announcing it was a girl, he asked, "Well, Cordie, what are you gonna name her?" And Mama answered, "I don't care **what** *you name her… just name her* the last!*" And that he did.*

When my sister, Julia Mae heard the story, she just laughed and said, "See, what I've been saying all along is true. I knew you were adopted." Just as an aside, we have learned that my father was much older than 58 years as recorded on my birth certificate, but he must have been at least 63 years of age. (The 1870 slave census listed him as a young child per Ancestry.com.) Funny. We think it's only women who fib about their age.

Mama told me that I probably weighed about 6 pounds, average length, and healthy. Oh, did I mention that none of these facts were on my certificate? But there was one more "shocker." Everybody expected that my skin tone would be ebony, but nobody was expecting a baby with my complexion to have reddish brown hair (more reddish than brown). Thus, advice swiftly came in from well-meaning neighbors and friends on how to remedy this situation. I was mortified when I learned that my hair was dyed by applying a mixture of coal oil and coffee grinds together. It appeared that after several months had passed, my hair was its *normal* color...black.

By the age of three, our family had moved to Louisville. I guess that was when I became aware that my father was sightless. Dad, or *Uncle Bob,* as he was called most often, was a retired fireman with the L & N Railroad Company. The word was that cinders popped in his eyes and blinded him. Therefore, he mostly just sat in an easy chair listening to the noises of the home while playing tunes on his harmonica. Mama had to shoulder the heaviest part in rearing me and my siblings—my brother, Ruben, called *Pete* after *Peter Rabbit,* was about 10 years old and my sister, Julia Mae, was close to seven years of age. My twin siblings, Maxine (*Maxie*) and Howard, nicknamed *Buckle, were* in their teens, while my older brother, Frank, and my oldest sibling, Donzella, were already out of the house and married. We all had nicknames or shortened forms of our name. I was addressed as Sue most of the time. Buckle came up with calling me Abigail and some called me Suzanna as in the song "Oh! Susanna" by Stephen Foster. I was on the fast track of knowing the significance of being called my full name by my mother. When she called out, "Sue An'nah!", I knew I was in big trouble and I was always getting into big trouble.

Memories have a habit of slipping away, especially those earlier ones; but, as I reflected backwards, I was surprised at how much of my past I could recall. I remember a lot about the first home I lived in after my family moved from my birthplace in Bloomfield to Louisville. The white frame *shotgun* house in the 1700 block of Dumesnil Street sure wasn't much to look at. One could stand in the front room and look straight through to the kitchen, thus the name "shotgun." It had no inside plumbing, only the outhouse in the back yard; water was drawn from the well for drinking, cooking, and bathing. There was a pot-bellied wood stove that served many purposes: cooking, heating, etc. I remember being warned not to go too close to it, but to only go close enough to keep warm.

My brothers had the chore of chopping wood, bringing it inside and putting it in its designated place. Maxine was Mama's assistant. We had to mind our manners around her or she would tell Mama all.

Our neighborhood was mostly residential with a grocery store on the corner. Oh yes... the corner store where I got my first lesson in the Ten Commandments... "Thou shall not steal." I just couldn't resist walking by that big juicy red apple just begging to go home with me. I picked it up and hurried out of the store, all the time knowing Mama would send me back to return it as quickly as I came. I had to go back to face the music, apologize, and offer to pay. The store owner was waiting for me as if he knew he'd only have to wait awhile. It was in this neighborhood that I sustained a minor concussion after being struck by a truck. I also got my first dog bite. There was a cute little puppy that I thought wouldn't hurt a flea. So, after being told several times that he had teeth, I put my finger in his mouth to find out. Yep! He had teeth and I've still have the scar from the five stitches I got for my ignorance.

In approximately two years, we had relocated to another house. It's somewhat strange that I don't remember as much about this one as I did the first house. However, this is where I lived when I underwent a catastrophic experience. I tried to extract these details and record them in this *Talk Story:*

WATER, WATER, EVERYWHERE!

I was four and a half years old when my hometown in Louisville, Kentucky experienced the great flood of the Ohio River. It was the winter of 1937 and it became a disaster that claimed almost 400 lives and left roughly one million people homeless across five states.

Being so young, the main thing I remember was the fear and anxiety pasted on my family members' faces. Along with the hustle and bustle of the authorities getting everyone to safety. The severity of the flood was lost on me. However, what I do remember was seeing the water rise up to the level of our second-floor window. I could see boats floating on what used to be our city streets. It was a very frightening sight which threw me into what was called a spasm or convulsion. When my mother saw me shaking uncontrollably, with only the whites of my eyes showing, she summoned a doctor who I was told came by boat to examine me. Yes, back in those days, doctors made house calls even during a flood. I guess that's one reason they were called "the good old days." After the diagnosis, he left instructions to try to keep me calm and it would most likely last a day or so.

I was told I didn't know anybody but my sister, Julia Mae, not even my parents and other siblings. Julia was the only one who could get me to eat or drink. However, we shortly had to be moved to a shelter. But we were not all taken to the same place. Pete got separated from the rest of the family and was taken to another shelter in town. My condition only made adjusting to the sleeping and dining arrangements in the shelter more difficult. Mother was a real trooper—taking care of me and praying for my recovery while worrying about her missing baby boy, not knowing if we'd ever see him again. Adding to all that was her supervision of my other four siblings, and caring my sightless father. Needless to say, we could use a miracle.

You can call it what you desire, but it appears to me this was exactly what we got…a miracle. There was a woman in the shelter who just came over to talk and to perhaps help in some way. When she was told what had happened to me and that it had now been over a week with no improvement, she asked my mother's permission to try an old remedy on me. Well, we didn't have anything to lose, so why not. She left our area and returning with a box of Morton's table salt. After raising my shirt and pouring salt on my stomach, she began to massage the area. Almost immediately, I came out of the trance, smiling and greeting people all around. Just like a child, all I wanted to do was to be turned loose to go play.

By the time I became old enough for kindergarten and first grade, I had never ventured out of my neighborhood. We didn't own a car and Mama never learned to drive. Anyway, Louisville had an excellent transit system. First, we had the street car and afterwards the bus. So, of course, I was unaware of segregation between whites and blacks (coloreds). Mama picked the seating area that was in the back with neighbors and friends. The only white person I had encountered previously was the man who owned the corner store. I later found out that he was Jewish. Mother took in laundry from white people so I would see them sometimes as they picked up their shirts and such.

Other times, she would board the bus and ride hours to get to their homes to do housecleaning. When she was not home, I knew to obey my older sister, but not so much Julia, whose job was to keep me out of trouble. Realizing she was gone so much, Mama made opportunities to spend quality time with all of us including my sightless father. The following *Talk Story* describes such an occasion:

THE INVISIBLE WHITE ONLY SIGN

One beautiful summer day, my mom and I took the street car to downtown Louisville. I remember she dressed me up in a pretty blue dress adorned with a huge bow in the back that she had made for me. And although my hair was quite short, that fact didn't hinder her from putting big blue ribbons on each braid with matching barrettes on each end.

We had shopped around the Kresge 5 & 10 Cents Store and was just about to leave when I noticed a little girl about my age sitting on a stool at what I now know was a soda fountain. She was dressed in a pretty red dress with a big red bow in the back just like mine. Her hair was long and light yellow with matching bows and barrettes on each of her plaits.

She seemed to really be enjoying swiveling around on a tall stool. I wanted to do that too. So I broke away from my mother's hand and took the empty stool next to her and began turning about just like my new-found friend was doing.

Before my mother could reach me, I was told very roughly to get up because I wasn't allowed to sit there. My mother then tenderly took my hand and led me away. With tears in her eyes, she gently explained why I was not allowed to sit and play on the bar stool.

I was six years old when I first became acquainted with racial discrimination.

Yes, but it surely wasn't the last. As I grew, I became more and more aware of the *Jim Crow* conditions that were practiced and accepted by colored people in my hometown. It was something you hated, but knew you had to get used to it. That's just the way it was. We all had to go along with it and stay in our place. That meant, among other things, riding in the back of the bus, drinking from water fountains clearly marked for coloreds, and eating in areas designated for you.

Times back in the 30s were so much different than they are today. There were rules to follow, both spoken and unspoken, and you'd best be knowing them. Rules, such as, "Children should be seen not heard; be still while I instill (meaning shut your mouth and listen) and don't ask why when I tell you something to do." I didn't like any of them! Looking back on my actions, I can see that I would be labeled *a strong-willed child.* I was definitely a challenge and God had given me just the person to handle it—my mother. How my mother who only had an 8th grade education knew then what psychologists know now, after years of in depth study, is mind-boggling. She simply gave me enough rope to hang myself hoping I would come out better on the other side of it.

In the spring of 1941, we moved from the area that had been flooded into a newly built public housing project—Beecher Terrace-1011 Liberty Court was the first complete address I can recall. Upon entering our new abode, many feelings merged together. Boy, was I ever excited! I had never seen a brand new apartment before and with all grand modern conveniences. There were shiny faucets that water came out of (both hot and cold) instead of a well, white smooth bathtubs, radiators that warmed the rooms, and tiled floors so shiny you could see your face in. And most importantly were the inside facilities: toilet that flushed with a holder for soft paper nearby. We had three bedrooms so we were no longer cramped up; however, we still had to share space with other siblings. The girls' bedroom had to hold the three of us. Mama put twin beds in our rooms assigning Maxine to one of them and me and Julia to the other. I was quite small so I could just about fit in anywhere.

Television had not come on the scene yet, but we had the radio. I loved the times our family spent huddled around the radio, not only listening but looking at it. Yes, we'd stare straight at the radio and the characters seemed to come alive--Amos and Andy, Filbert McGee and Mollie, and The Shadow, just to name a few. And then there were the times when the radio went silent and Mama would tell stories of the past. She would dramatize them in such an exciting way, sometimes with singing like that included in this Talk Story that was published in Troy State University's Copper Blade Review, 2002.

AN IMPROMPTU SOLOIST

Every Saturday evening my family would gather around the kitchen table and listen to the older ones tell tall tales of their past. Some were serious, but most were funny. A pot of hot coffee was brewed to accompany the cookies, while the children enjoyed a cold glass of milk. It was important to get within a sufficient hearing range, so that nothing would slip pass us. For this reason, every piece of loose furniture was crowded around the table. My mother was usually the star attraction. She had survived two husbands, Daddy Frank and Uncle Bob, and had amassed a number of good stories. Daddy Frank would be the centerpiece of this yarn

The night my mother told of an uninvited guest soloist at a church service was both funny and bizarre. She painted a vivid picture of the church setting, the congregation, and the scene where the soloist appeared.

"Ours was like any other rural town in Kentucky where people worked hard all day in anticipation of relaxing in the evening. There wasn't much going on in the way of entertainment; however, you did have a choice. You could take your pick of either going to church or to the local bar. Our town had two churches—one Baptist and one Methodist. We had a circuit preacher that held services at the Baptist church on the first and third Sundays and at the Methodist church on the second and fourth Sundays. But none of that really mattered because the church-going crowd would attend both churches.

Bloomfield Baptist Church was having its spring revival, and all the saints would be there. The small white-framed church was of simple structure without all the comforts we have today. There was no air-conditioning; the cooling was provided by a huge electric fan that stood humming loudly in the corner of the church. The unscreened windows were raised, allowing the breeze to flow in and the voices to go out, so when church was in session, everybody for miles around would know it. The hour had come for the services to begin.

As the congregation gathered, you could feel the anticipation and see the excitement on each face. The Deacons had warmed up the church even more than the outside temperature with the singing of hymns and fervent prayers intermingled with heart-felt testifying. The members of the Mother's Board were seated in their usual places all adorned in white. Meanwhile, the Evangelist was waiting anxiously like a boxer anticipating the opening bell. He would have his turn, after the rendering of one more Negro spiritual. At this point in her tale, Mother would start singing a verse and chorus of "Get on Board, Little Children." She sang: "The gospel train is comin', It's comin' round the bend; And if you want to git on, repent of all yo sins. Then you can git on board, lil' chillun, Git on board, lil' chillun, Git on board, lil' chillun, Dere's room for plenty of mo."

Just as we had completed singing the first verse and chorus, we were astonished at what took place next. It seems that Daddy Frank had made his way home, after drinking all the liquor his stomach could hold, and found himself locked out of the house. He heard the singing and shouting over at the church and knew exactly where the keys were—with me in my apron pocket.

Suddenly, all eyes were fixed on the left window of the church where there was some of disturbance going on. Was it a bat hitting against the sill? Was it a bird trying to get into the church?

No! It was Daddy Frank peering through the open window, clearing his throat, and preparing to convey a message in song. He had arrived on the scene just as the congregation had finished singing the last line of the chorus when he roared out these words. "And if my wife is in tha, you kin tell her for me, she can git on board if she wants ta, but send me the kitchen key."

Undoubtedly, Mother left the revival meeting that night not feeling very revived. She had gone to church to hear a word from the Lord, but instead had been treated to a "not-so-beautiful" solo.

Even though his actions were deviant, Daddy Frank's antics displayed some bona fide talent. Whenever I recount this story, I am dumbfounded at how easily he composed the lyrics with which he communicated, in addition to having those

22

lyrics rhyme. *We have all heard it said that "a mind is a terrible thing to waste." Is it possible Daddy Frank could have been a forerunner of Dr. Seuss or James Weldon Johnson?*

Each Sunday after church service, the entire family would gather around Mom's dinner table and share in a delicious, home-cooked meal. This tradition will always remain at the top of my most enjoyable occasions.

We were just getting comfortable in our brand-new surroundings when in an instance our peace and tranquility was shattered. I recorded my reactions in this *Talk Story:*

SAFELY HOME

I was just a nine-year-old kid when Japanese planes attacked the U.S. Naval Base at Pearl Harbor in Hawaii. Over 2,400 Americans lost their lives that day. President Franklin D. Roosevelt is recorded to say that this would be "a day which will live in infamy." The attack on Pearl Harbor immediately galvanized a divided nation into action. Of course at that time, I couldn't foresee the effect both events would personally have on me. What I do remember about that day, December 7, 1941, are the sounds, the tears, and the whispering that went on around me. In a futile effort, grown-ups in my family were trying their best to shield and protect my heart and spirit. All the while, radios were blasting the news, church bells were ringing, and people were weeping. I knew that something mighty serious was happening, and it was. America was propelled into World War II within days. I would soon see my two older brothers, Ruben and Howard drafted into the Army and placed in the midst of battle. My eldest brother, Frank, was exempt since he was married with about five of the ten children he would eventually father. Through this whole ordeal, I remember seeing my mother on her knees faithfully praying for God's protection. They were both in the heat of battle but they returned home safely.

From six years on until about my twelfth birthday, I was quite tom-boyish. I loved to play all the sports that boys played…baseball, football, and such. However, what I enjoyed most was climbing. I'd leap at any challenge to display my ability. The housing projects where we lived had basketball courts in area playgrounds where mainly boys would go to play. I would be right there with them. When one of them gave a dare, I was all in. One day, an older boy who was taller than the others, laid out the details of a double dare. Keep in mind that the basketball hoop was the standard height of 10 feet with another 3 feet for the backboard. We were to climb up the back portion of the poles, climb over the top of the backboard, and drop ourselves through the 10 foot hoop (net had been long gone by now) to the ground. No problem. If they could do, so could I. This was the first of many times that would follow. Another time, we'd jump at a height equal to 20 plus steps to a 4 X 4 foot landing instead of taking the stairs down. I loved to push the envelope, so to speak.

Mother was offered a way to channel some of my energies into something useful and beneficial to my development. My aunt and uncle invited me to spend the summer months on their farm in Bloomfield with them and my two cousins. How exciting this was for a city slicker like me! Pigs, cows, chickens and worms— yes; worms, here I come! I knew I'd have to rough it, and not have all those conveniences I was used to in the city, but I was ready. Aunt Corine laid out the pattern I'd follow for years to come while visiting them. I was given certain chores and responsibilities that were mine alone to complete which was no different than ones at home. Use your imagination as I introduce you to me through the eyes of a bull. I rewrote this story for an assignment through the Val McGee's Writers' Forum. The assignment was to write a page or two from an animal's point of view. My animal's name in this *Talk Story* is Stud.

THE RUNNING OF THE BULL

Introduction:

Oh-way o-nay! ere-Hay e-shay omes-cay again-way! ust-May I-way ave-hay o-tay ut-pay up-way ith-way is-thay every-way ummer-say? I-way ew-knay e-shay as-way ouble-tray as-way oon-say as-way I-way aid-lay y-may eyes-way on-way er-hay. I-way uess-gay it-way as-way y-may intuitive-way ind-may at-way ork-way. If-way only-way I-way ew-knay ow-hay o-tay onverse-cay ith-way er-hay, erhaps-pay e-way ould-cay e-bay iends-fray. ut-Bay at-whay anguage-lay an-cay I-way earn-lay o-tay ommunicate-cay ith-way er-hay. y-May iend-fray, oooie-Say e-thay ig-pay, agreed-way o-tay each-tay e-may is-hay anguage-lay, ecause-bay e-hay ew-knay ots-lay of-way umans-hay at-thay oke-spay it-way. o-Say ooie-Say ave-gay e-may a-way ash-cray ourse-cay in-way "Pig Latin" in-way ich-whay ow-nay I-way am-way ery-vay illful-skay. y-May ory-stay ill-way emonstrate-day ow-hay y-may intuition-way about-way about-way is-thay ittle-lay isitor-vay as-way ight-ray on-way arget-tay.

English translation of Introduction

Oh no! Here she comes again! Must I have to put up with this every summer? I knew she was trouble as soon as I

25

laid my eyes on her. I guess it was my intuitive mind at work. If only I knew how to converse with her, perhaps we could be friends. But what language can I learn to communicate with her? My friend, Sooie the pig, agreed to teach me his language, because he knew lots of humans that spoke it. So Sooie gave me a crash course in "Pig Latin" in which now I am very skillful. My story will demonstrate how my intuition about this little visitor was right on target.

The bull's point of view...

About this time each year, a little girl comes to the country to visit her Aunt Corine and Uncle Ray. They are very fine folk with gentle spirits who take good care of their farm and farm animals. Everybody calls me "Stud." I am the only bull in the pen with 10 cows, so you see they need me to be and stay on top of my game. All was well until this young girl came from the big city of Louisville to experience life on the farm.

I soon discovered that this one didn't like to follow rules and thought nothing of challenging each one them. The first day on the farm, she was given a tour with instructions of what she could and could not do. Susie was told that life on the farm can be fun, but it can also be dangerous. I overheard Aunt Corine give her several warnings. She said specifically, "Do not go close to the pen where Stud is fenced. He does not like red, so avoid going close to him wearing red or carrying anything red." I quickly understood that saying "no" to her was the same as saying "yes!"

My pen was located about 20 feet or so away from the outhouse. I prayed that the family would have some other means of relieving themselves, like a slop jar, but that was just wishful thinking. It wasn't long before little Susie had to 'go'. I noticed that she didn't have to use it too badly, because the

26

first thing she did was to come by and tease me. Susie had made a flag out of a limb and tied a red piece of cloth on its end. She used it to poke at me through the fence. I could tell she got a kick out of hearing me snort and such snorting I did. I give her this credit though; she had what you humans call 'stick-to-it-ness' I think. This behavior would continue each and every day. I said to myself, "One-way ay-day, ittle-lay usie-Say, you're oing-gay o-tay ub-ray e-may e-thay ong-wray ay-way or-fay e-thay ast-lay ime-tay." Translation: One day, little Susie, you're going to rub me the wrong way for the last time."

I was definitely angry and frustrated, but not disheartened. I waited patiently for her next visit, thinking… "Every bull has his day and a good bull may have two." Just about then, Susie came bouncing along without a care in the world and heading my way. What? Today she is making a run for the outhouse. My golden opportunity has arrived!

I quickly moved to the far side of the pen so as to get a running start. With all the steam I could muster up, I jumped over the fence. There I stood waiting for little Susie and I to meet up close and personal. The door to the outhouse opens and to Susie's surprise, there I stood…digging my feet into the dirt and snorting--making her favorite sounds. I could see the panic in her eyes and could hear her saying, "Wat to do? Wat to do?!? She quickly closed the door to the outhouse while she constructed a plan of escape. I'm not sure what she had in mind, because I had her cornered.

This girl was indeed a city-slicker. Since she had been privy to going to those movie theaters, she recalled a scene that she thought would be her salvation. Susie remembered that time after time when someone was wanting to get away from their pursuer, they would take off running as fast as they *could. However, they wouldn't run in a straight line, they would always run in a circle while making the circle wider and wider, bigger and bigger each time. That's exactly what she did.*

Susie ran and circled the outhouse several times with me right on her track. Then when she had what she thought was enough space between us, she headed for the kitchen door and beat me to the porch by a hair. I stood their pouting about my missed chance of payback saying, "I-way id-day ot-nay atch-cay er-hay is-thay ime-tay, ut-bay ou-yay an-cay e-bay ure-say I-way ill-way ext-nay ear-yay!" Translation: "I did not catch her this time, but you can be sure I will next year."

When I came back home after my summer visit, I didn't miss a beat. I just had to focus my attention elsewhere. Mama trusted me to stay at home with my father at various times while she did day work. That proved to be very beneficial to me and my friends. It became an opportunity for a party--one that my father could not detect. As they filed in, I warned them to be extremely quiet and to not to make a sound. It, we thought, was just a little harmless fun. When Dad would ask what I was doing or what was that noise, I lied. It's hard to believe that sometimes this would go on for hours. The house was always back in its original condition when they left…no harm, no foul, at least that what I thought. However, my payday was coming. I was 10 years old when my father died. And did I ever have a hard time during the funeral service. It seemed that every little lie and mischievous act I had hidden from his "sightless" eyes came flooding back to my memory. I recognized it for what it was—guilt. I could hear my voice saying over and over, "Lord, I'm so sorry; please forgive me." I later confessed what I had done to my mother and asked her forgiveness. She told me that I should pray and ask the Lord to save me. I wasn't quite sure what that meant, but I knew I needed to modify my behavior. Several months passed before

I asked Jesus to come into my heart and He did. I was 12 years old when I was baptized at the church I had attended since I was a child, Central Baptist Church. Through attending Sunday School and other Christian involvements, I became more knowledgeable of God's word and wanted desperately to follow it. I began observing what other Christians were doing to honor and glorify God. To my dismay, I learned that some people were only pretending to follow Him out of tradition. Here is an example.

ONLY BLUE-VEINED NEED APPLY

"After the Civil War, the divisions created during enslavement led to divisions based on differences in skin color, hair texture and physical appearance. These early laws and practices took root and eventually influenced several parts of Black life." (Jackson-Lowman)

That is why an announcement such as the one indicated above could have been printed and hung on the front door of the Quinn Chapel CME (Colored Methodist Episcopal) in my hometown. By the age of twelve, I had become accustomed to the white only or colored only signs, but to be further discriminated against was, to say the least, degrading. I learned at an early age that there were degrees to which one could be 'colored'.

My immediate family was comprised of those that ran the gamut in skin tone from as ebony as coal to as pale as a sheet. It didn't bother us one bit. We loved each other and that love made us oblivious of the differences of our hues. Because my skin tone was that of a dark chocolate, I was told by other people outside of my family what activities I could or could not participate in, even within my own race. I got that and was taught to obey certain restrictions. However, one would not expect this humiliation to reach into the church, but it did.

At Quinn Chapel CME Church only light-colored Blacks would be eligible for membership. It had nothing to do with "whosoever will, let him come." The blue-veined test had to be administered before you could apply. It was simple enough and painless, physically. So, to become of part of that church, one would have to roll up his sleeve and show his veins. If the committee members could readily see his veins, he was in and if not… oh well.

Ironically enough, I had two brothers and two sisters that would have been eligible, but not me. I definitely could not have passed that test or any other of the tests administered back then. There was the "brown bag test" where membership was denied if your skin was darker than a paper grocery bag. Some churches painted their doors light brown; a signal to those darker than the door that they were not welcome. And the "kinky hair test" where a comb had to run smoothly through one's hair without snagging. In some cases, churches hung a comb at their doors indicating that only those with hair textures like Whites could enter. (Jackson-Lowman 2013). These were shameful acts that promoted more segregation than that was legally ordered.

During my preteens and teen years, I still struggled with being deceitful and untruthful. Mother did not have an age limit on administering corporal punishment—spanking. We all knew that as long as we were under her roof, we were expected to obey her rules with no questions asked. I vividly recall my last spanking from Mama. I had begged her to let me have a party for my 12th birthday and she agreed with these stipulations: no rowdiness, no alcohol, and no dirty dancing. There was a reason why she warned "no dirty dancing." The following *Talk Story* will make it all plain.

BOOGYING DOWN

I loved to dance and my sister, Julia, did not, so that little detail presented a perfect opportunity for me to go along with her to older teen parties with Mom's approval. Julia was a beautiful, but a little heavyweight; I was lean, but shapely. I think that caused her to be a little shy; while on the other hand, I was both outgoing and not a bit shy. Mama wanted Julia to go out more and socialize with others her age, so she allowed me to accompany her to parties and such. Her friends welcomed me with open arms (so to speak) because they knew that I loved to dance, especially to do the boogie woogie!

Boogie Woogie was a style of music in the 30's that was similar to jazz or blues. It was played on the piano with a fast, strong, steady beat. It was like dancing to rock music today.

My birthday was coming up soon so I begged Mama to let me have a party for my 12th birthday. I had my fingers crossed that she'd say yes. As you know I hadn't done anything that deserved her approval. She gave her permission with one condition. "Okay. But I don't want to see any of that dirty dancing from you that I've heard about. Do you understand?" I said, "I promise, Mama."

The party started with about 11 other friends present. Mom had cooked up plenty of treats and the celebration was relatively quiet and contained until someone put in a 45 rpm on the Victrola phonograph record player. It was a favorite entitled, "Boogie Woogie Bugle Boy." My 'boyfriend' grabbed my hand and we hit the floor. You can say, we cleared the floor. Everyone that had been dancing moved aside so we could have more room to strut our stuff. He swung me out, turned me around, and pulled me back to him. Everything was going well until the record was nearly at its end. When he threw me back this time, I dropped to the floor and eased myself up to him in a very sexual maneuver. Just as I was just about up to him, I ran into my mom's hand across my face. She firmly announced, "The party's over!"

It wasn't the end of my dancing career, but it was definitely over that night.

No one could understand why I could eat so much and not gain a pound. I figured it was because I was very active. Along with sports and other activities, I really like to skate and did so often at our neighborhood skating rink. The rink gave me another chance to dance on skates. But my eating habit was not normal as noted in the following *Talk Story*.

LOVE THAT FRIED CHICKEN

Fried chicken was absolutely my favorite food in the world when I was young. I loved it then and still do! My love for it showed in every bite I would savor. So much so that my mother let me eat a whole chicken (10 pieces) on Sunday providing I'd eat my vegetables first. Unknowingly, at that time I had an overactive thyroid problem which allowed me to eat a large amount of food without gaining weight. So when fried

32

chicken was on the Sunday menu, I'd get a helping of all the veggies and then tear into "my chicken." Mama gave me the option of eating it all then or saving some until later. She gave me a strong, clear admonishment that I could NOT have any more fried chicken for the rest of the day, although there was always plenty left on the stove top in a covered roaster.

One Sunday after evening church service, I began to reminisce about the leftover chicken--thinking I'd die if I didn't get one more piece of that warm, juicy bird. So I rushed home ahead of Mama and a lady friend with whom she was walking to grab a leg and gulp it down unnoticed. She wouldn't miss one little piece. Just as I was enjoying the sumptuous leg, I heard Mama coming up the steps. And she was coming fast! Now I was too greedy to throw the leg in the trashcan, so I rolled it across the floor. All the while I was thinking it would roll under the radiator and I'd let it stay there until Mama left the room and then retrieve it. Wrong!

To my surprise, the chicken leg could not roll smoothly due to the bites I had taken out of it. So, as Mama looked on with disgust, it rolled in slow motion across the floor like a man walking with a limp. Punishment was dealt out appropriately. I might add that this was before enactment of all those child abuse laws (smile).

World War II ended on August 15, 1945 and my two brothers returned home soon afterwards. What a joyous celebration we had! Mama had prayed earnestly for their safe return and they had made it. However, they had witnessed many of their comrades that were not so fortunate.

Buckle held the record for the biggest eater in the family and had heard that I was a close second. Subsequently, everyone knew there would have to be a contest to declare a winner once and for all. It was on! He couldn't let his 13 year old sister beat him at eating. So, we agreed to see which one of us could eat the most of Mama's pancakes. Her pancakes were so light they had to be held down with lots of butter and syrup. The rules of the contest were decided upon. Mama would be the judge.

We began with our plate lined with sausage patties around the rim. Mama would fix four pancakes at a time and after consuming the four, we'd raise our hand indicating that we wanted four more.

We both ate 4 pancakes. He raised his hand for 4 more and so did I. That was 8. Buckle raised his finger for 4 more and so did I. That made 12. I raised my hand for 4 more and so did my brother…that totaled 16. However, when he lifted his hand for 4 more…I had to drop out. The score was 16 to 20. Mama just laughed and called us foolish—and we were.

Mama always was our most fervent encourager. She knew how hard it was for her to provide financially for her family and did not want us to undergo the same fate. Therefore, she did all she could to inspire us. She would say to us, "You can be anything you want to be." Words cannot express the faith it must have taken to say those particular words of reassurance in the segregated society in which we lived. But, that reality didn't stop her, because she gleaned her strength from God's Word. One of her favorite Bible verses that was passed down throughout our family was drilled into us. "I can do all things through Christ who strengthens me." *Philippians 4:13*. Mama's challenge included studying hard in school and it carried over into piano practice when I began taking piano lessons.

The name, Bourgard School of Music and Art, sounds impressive, and it was. All genre of music and art was taught there. Mama wanted me to be introduced to the arts. So much so that she paid an equivalent of one day's wages to give me one-half hour piano lessons every week. The only prerequisite was that I faithfully go take my lessons and that I'd practice diligently. Practicing wasn't a problem, but going to the site proved to be. My mode of travel was the Louisville Transit System. I could catch the bus a block away from my house and it let me off a block away from the building. Here's the problem...the girl who took lessons before me always took her dog and of course, he had to wait outside on the porch. I had a great fear of dogs—all kinds, big or small—that never left me since I was bitten by that puppy before I was six. Adding to the dilemma was the realization that her younger brother took his lesson following me. That meant the dog was not going anywhere. The only decision I could safely make was to skip the lesson and return home to explain. Wrong choice. When word got back to Mama's ears, she was not a happy camper. She would not hear of it and asked, "Have you thought of making friends with the dog and his owner? He might just be a friendly as you." I took Mama's advice and ended up completing several more years of piano.

My first paid position as a "musician" was for the Sunday School assembly at my church. I had been taking music lessons for 2 years and had mastered most of the familiar tunes from our hymnbook, at least I thought I had. I can recall how difficult it was the very first time I attempted to play the piano with an audience singing along. It was frightening and I was so nervous! My eyes filled with water thereby making the notes blurry, my legs shook so hard that I had to use one of my hands to steady them, and the congregation's voices and my music definitely was not in sync. You can imagine my surprise when I heard the thundering roar of "Amens" and applaud coming from the assembly. I remember feeling, "Maybe '*I can do all things through Christ who strengthens.*' "

Buckle and Pete moved out on their own leaving only four at home when I reached my high school years. I continued to play for the church and eventually became Youth Choir Director. Boys did not have my complete attention until a family started attending who had a teenaged son who could really sing. He was younger than I, so I directed my attention elsewhere (for a short time anyway). There was this classmate of mine who rode the school bus from his house that was 20 miles or so from Central Colored High School where I attended. It was the only colored school within a radius of 25 miles making my friend, Charles, having to be bused pass several all-white schools to get to the black one. This was his daily routine, but on Wednesday he had his parents' permission to stay in town after school. Shortly, he asked me if I would go to the movie theater with him and after getting my mother's okay, I said, "Yes." Charles was quite interesting in that he always wore one *green wool glove* on his left hand. Nothing was wrong with the hand; it was an attention-getter. The teachers just overlooked it, since it did not interfere with his studies.

Charles was not the only boy I dated. I went out to sports events with some others and to parties with a selected few. Mama observed my popularity, but as long as I ran with the *right* crowd, she trusted my judgment. Then came the day that I witnessed my mother crying and sobbing in a way I'd never seen before. No, not even when my brothers went off to war.

"Julia Mae is pregnant", Mother said with a broken heart. That statement ushered in a major decision time for me, and led me to vow that I would not get do the same. Julia quit high school right before she was to graduate with her friends. It was 1949 and that was the way things were back then. Girls who got pregnant could not graduate, but the boys who impregnate them could.

It was a baby boy, Larry Eugene, who would knock me out of my, *I'm the baby role, and I loved it.* The sounds emanating from our newest member of the family were magical, to say the least. Unfortunately, his life would be cut off early. The doctors diagnosed him with leukemia at 15 years of age and he died at 16 on the 4th of July. Boy, how was he loved! He touched more people in his short lifetime than many do living to a ripe old age.

I did keep the promise I made that day to my mother and graduated from Central Colored High School in June,

1950. Although I kept my grade point average with in the top ten percent of my class, college was not a viable option for me. Scholarships were in short demand; my family did not have the money; and, there was still a *class system* present. It was unwritten, but thoroughly understood. I'm talking about the division perpetrated by many that excluded darker skinned blacks from participating equally with those of lighter complexions.

The only alternative I had if I wanted to attend college was to work and save for it. After I secured my birth certificate, I secured employment at the Enro Shirt Factory in Louisville. The money I earned was monitored closely by my mom. We just couldn't spend our earning anyway we desired. No way! Some of it went to assisting with household expenses, some went to clothing and other personal expenses, and a set amount went into savings. There was not much left to blow after all was divvied up. But, you know, it worked, and I learned a valuable lesson about finances that would stay with me until this day. When the opportunity came, I enrolled in St. Helena's Commercial College and successfully completed the required course. It wasn't my first choice of a teaching degree, but I would not know at this time what effect this attainment would have on me in the future.

PART II

MY MARRIAGE TO TOMMY

Soon, I found myself drawn to a young man who had come to our church a few years back, even though I knew he was younger than I. However, as the years passed by and we

were constantly thrown into close association with each other, we soon felt that the difference in our ages was not a factor. Thomas Davis had joined the membership of Central Baptist Church, where I attended, along with his aunt and uncle who had legal custody of him. We were involved in all the youth and young adult activities. Tommy had a great singing voice and he became a vital part of the music department. We really became close and it wasn't long before everyone thought of us as a couple. Whenever you'd see one, you would see the other. Naturally, the idea of marriage was in the forefront of practically all of the older members' mind, and it wasn't far from ours either.

Need I say more? We fell in love and was married in July, 1954. I was carrying our first child, although, this was not the reason for our marriage. The most obvious ones were that we just couldn't keep away from each other, and that it was the right thing to do. Everybody threw their arms around us and encouraged us in so many ways. Tommy worked very hard to provide for us. Although the work as a stockman didn't pay that much, it was enough for the three of us to make ends meet. We lived with his mother, Mama Lamb and step-father, Popsie for a short period. Our first child was a girl born December, 1954 and we named her Deborah Ann and called her by a shortened version, Debbie. It was the most popular name for a girl born in the '50s, mainly due to the popularity of actress/singer Debbie Reynolds.

Debbie was about 6 months old when we moved into *our own place*—a small two bedroom apartment. The good part was that we had finally gotten to a place financially where we could survive on our own. The bad part was the sharing of one bathroom with all the other residents in the building. Because I was pregnant again, we secured a slop bucket that was used as a toilet to reduce frequent trips up and down the stairs. On Saturdays we'd go to Mama's and take soaking baths that would have to last us until the next Saturday.

Keith Clayton was born later that year on December, 14th. I wanted to name him Thomas, Jr. especially since he was born on his father's birthday, but he won out explaining that he was a junior himself. So, Keith was given his father's middle name, Clayton. Needless to say, we were happy to have two healthy children—a girl and a boy, but neither of us planned to have more any time soon. (Remember, this was before the pill.)

We had presently outgrown that small 2-room apartment, so we began searching for a larger place. When we applied for public housing, the manager of Beecher Terrace told us she only had a three-room apartment available. Then she took one look at us and let us have the larger one thinking that more children would be forthcoming. We were grateful but surely didn't want more children anytime soon. Shortly after Keith was born, Mama began advising how to control the number of children we wanted. Mama would say, "Name it the Last." It worked for her when she named me *the last*.

By May of 1957, our third child was born but not without Mama's suggesting a name for our newborn. She's say, "Remember, name him *the last*." Glenn Eric entered our world with a bang. He was born on my mother's couch in her living room, all 8 lbs. of him. However, he was a very welcome addition to our little family. I couldn't help thinking of the housing manager's words to us last year. We really needed a 3-bedroom apartment now that we had two boys and a girl.

Anybody observing us would say that we were an ideal young family trying to rear our children in a Christian environment. Tommy was attentive to my every desire and showed me he meant the words he had written on the back of his photograph.

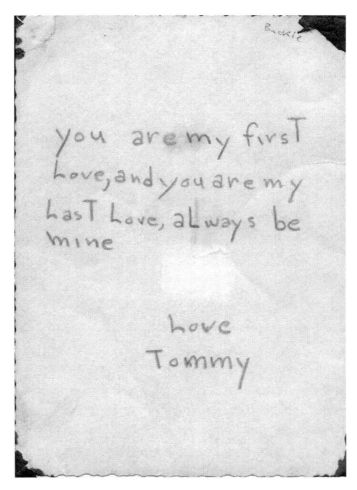

you are my first love, and you are my last love, always be mine

Love
Tommy

    We continued to be involved in Bible studies and choir. At home, Tommy and I continued to share the household chores after putting in a full work day. Every morning we would pack our youngsters up and take them to Mama for care.

    Soon, it became a time when we both felt that all we did revolved around the children. Therefore, when Tommy brought up the suggestion of both of us have a night out once a week, I agreed to it. I'd stay home with the kids while he went out with the boys and he'd babysit while I went out with the girls.

Our fourth child was conceived during this period of what we thought was a milestone in our marriage—one of mutual understanding on the subject of leisure time. Mama's words still rang loudly in my ears, (although by now you know I had a hearing problem). Mama said, again, "Whether it's a girl or boy, name it *the last*." Delphia Maxine (called Del) was born in March, 1959. My time out with the girls became less and less frequent because of my obligation with our small children. On the other hand, Tommy was picking up his pace and gaining some new-found freedoms that included alcohol consumption. What I didn't know then and would not know until later is that we were both having our nights out with the girls.

Looking back now, I wonder how I could have missed all the obvious signs, such as, his nights out becoming more frequent and the smell of alcohol on his breath which he said was from having a couple of beers. I guess the old saying is true: we only see what we want to see. Before we could enter into conversation that would perhaps change the course where we were heading, the bottom fell out and my happy world literally fell apart. I was expecting reconciliation, not this.

One Saturday night as I was going across the courtyard to my mother's apartment to borrow an item, I got the shock of my life. Who did I run into but my husband, Tommy, and his "lady"? They were just as shocked to see me as I was to see them. What are the odds of this happening? That I would be coming out of my apartment at the same time they would be walking up.

I stood there stunned at first, and then asked what was going on as if I could not see. I could see very plainly. She had to be at least eight months pregnant. And if that wasn't hurtful enough, he said, "Let me have you meet my next wife." As you can imagine, I was furious, but heartbroken. I did not see this coming. All I could do was to slap his face as hard as I could, and I'm sure there were a few choice words used. I do remember wishing I knew some *good curse words*. I would tell them off! I didn't go to Mom's house that night. Instead, I went back to our apartment and cried my heart out. After what seemed endless hours, I fell asleep knowing that my world had been utterly shattered.

The next morning, Tommy packed his belongings and moved out. It was over. Five years of marriage that *I* felt were happy ones. Now I had to figure out where my four little children and I would go from here. Delphia was only two-weeks old.

Even though I thought I had been hurt beyond repair, I couldn't deny the fact that I still loved him and wanted him back. The children missed him too, and they never let a day go by without asking me why their daddy was not home. How can anyone explain these matters to children four years of age and under?

The Court ordered child support for us in the amount of $10 per week for each child. I was grateful for any help no matter how small it was, since I had no other means of providing for our children. Receiving welfare assistance had always been looked down on in my family. We believed in working hard to support our families; hence, I was the first family member to do so. But, I had to swallow my pride for my kids' sakes.

Everyone continued to tell me that he would come back home after he saw the mistake he'd made. They assured me that this was just a phase and I wanted so much to believe them. After about two months had passed, telephone calls from Tommy began. First, it was to see how the children were doing. Something he had shown no interest in before, but wanting so badly to believe him, I was blindly led into his trap.

The next few days were filled with apologies, followed close by was the request to return home. What can I say? This is what I'd been waiting to hear…and I opened my heart and home to him again. For a couple of months our home was filled with joyful sounds of family life again. Daddy was home! It seemed so stupid to keep getting taken in by his lies and promises, but sometimes it takes a boulder to knock sense into our heads. In retrospect, either my head was really hard or my heart was very soft.

It wasn't long before our happy reunion produced another child, a son. I wish I could tell you that Tommy and I were both overjoyed. No. Emotions were surely lop-sided. His mind and heart was somewhere else. Time was up. It was time for him to return to the "other woman." Tommy and Lena's first child had been born and he had just been spending time with me until she was "well enough for sex."

So I returned to the Court once more. This time to add another $10 for support our fifth child, Rodney Wade, (again not named the last) who was born on April 3, 1960. The City Welfare Department threw in another $66.00. Things would be tight but with Tommy's $50 and the City's $66 we could survive.

Tommy ending up paying only two weeks of his legally obligated child support to the tune of $100 total. He left town and never gave his five children another thought or penny. So the income of $116 a month immediately dwindled down to $66.00 a month. Twenty-eight dollars of it went for rent. The math is easy; thirty-eight dollars had to last the six of us for an entire month. Still, we always had a sufficient amount of food, thanks to my sister, Donzella, who worked at a Catholic Home. She supplied us with bread, donuts, and sweet rolls. Local grocery stores would sale their bakery items to the public after having them one day on their shelves to "day old" bakeries who would keep them for about two more days before giving them to the Catholic Home who would then offer them to their workers in a day of so. We were so glad to see my sister come bringing all those goodies. Yes, they were a little stale, but freshened back up in the oven with welfare margarine spread heavily on them. Of course, other family members joined Donzella in just one of many doors that were opened to us in love. I would be neglectful, if I didn't mention how helpful Tommy's mother, (Mama Lamb), and his step-father, George, (lovingly called, Popsie) were. He didn't own a car-only a bicycle-but he would regularly ride 15 city blocks to bring us food.

Many nights I cried myself to sleep wondering what in the world was I going to do with these five precious ones looking to me for care. I knew they didn't know what was happening in their little world, but I did. I was never one to keep my head buried in the sand, so to speak. Being a careful observer of news, statistics, and trends caused me to know what *they* were saying. The year was 1960 and Social Science stats showed that odds were high that my sons would end up in prison and my daughters pregnant outside of marriage. This scared me to the max. Nobody in my family had ever been divorced and here I am--separated and singly rearing five small children. Bottom line: we couldn't have made it without the Lord, family, and a host of good friends. And that we had. I will never forget a dear minister encouraging me with these words, "Your home is not broken; it's just badly bent." As I moved forward into the unknown future, I've held on to those words for dear life.

My mother's teachings sprang up in my mind anew. She'd warn me saying, "You are the parent. Love on your children, but let them have no doubt that you are in control of the home. Never break a promise even when it comes to dealing out punishment for misbehaving. Above all, raise them up to love and fear the Lord. Don't let your children see you do anything that you may one day have to correct them about." I knew very well what she meant by those words. She mainly spoke of my not having male friends spend that night in our home, warning me if I do, I will not have grounds to speak up when my daughters want to repeat my actions.

Things began looking up for us right before Christmas when the long-awaited ADC (Aid to Dependent Children) check arrived…$132.00. I shouted, "Wow!" That was double what we had been surviving on for the last six months. I was definitely grateful, but I knew better to overspend. The City sponsored Christmas toys for underprivileged children. So, leaving the children in the care of Mama, I went to participate for the first time in a community toy drive. To my surprise, I entered a large spacious building which was very orderly. They found my name on the list and told me that I needed to find the age-appropriate gift for each of my five children. I was instructed that each child would receive one new toy, one slightly used toy, and as many as desired in the very used pile. I chose one from each patch since we already had an established rule of three toys max for Christmas. Christmas that year would be a turning point for family; we finally had enough money coming in to meet our financial needs. However, as the children grew, so did expense for their care. I certainly had my hands full with many daunting obligations facing me.

But I wasn't alone because Maxie stepped up to assist as only she could do. She was an unmarried practical nurse who willingly supplied nice clothes and accessories for all of my children. She made no difference between the boys and girls, however it was the girls who were privy to staying with her and Mama every Saturday night. Maxie was very meticulous about order. She had a distinctive place for everything. There was a ribbon drawer where she stored them all pressed, an underwear drawer, and a place for hankies. Nothing was out of place. Their Aunt Maxie had a special place in their lives that even grandma couldn't fill. My girls weren't the only ones who stayed on Saturdays, Julia Mae's girls stayed, too. However, we have all tasted her famous hamburgers, which were uniquely prepared in her distinct manner. Over the years, we have tried to perfect her burger; some of us have come close. We've even named them-- *Aunt Maxie's hamburger*. And boy, were they good! She would make them into quarter pound patties that had been seasoned perfectly, smother them with lots of steamed onions, add dill pickles, mustard/ketchup and maybe a slice of cheese. What set it off was her placing opened hamburger buns over the sautéed onions and letting them steam in the juice. (Another term for grease) Ooh, they were so good!

Debbie, my oldest child, began to take on responsibilities beyond her years and proved to be a great help to me. We still lived in the housing projects so our rent didn't increase. I was thankful for that. Even though she was too young to understand fully, I found myself sharing and asking for her input. Here's what she recalls.

WHITE, GREEN AND PINK PAPER

I remember my first lessons in problem solving and my introduction into handling family resources. At the age of five, I knew what bills were and knew how we paid them. Mama would collect wrinkled green paper in crisp white envelopes that she wrote on with a freshly knife sharpened pencil. Periodically, I remember a man would knock on our screen door announcing with a thundering voice that he was the "Insurance Man". He would need no announcement really because the news of his arrival in the housing projects would spread quickly by children running home to alert their parents of his impending arrival. Mama would greet him with a smile and would give him some wrinkled green paper from one of her crisp white envelopes. As a side note: the premiums paid on that policy helped pay for my wedding.

During my first financial lesson, open and unopened envelopes of varying colors were scattered all over the kitchen table that was adorned with a shiny but cold silver-fluted trim. Five and wise beyond my years, I was keenly aware that Mommy was sad and weighted under financial distress. I wanted to help so I asked, "What's wrong, Mama?" She explained that she had lots of bills but very little money to pay them with. While explaining her plight, mama slowly counted the wrinkled green papers that she pulled from the crisp white envelopes over and over again. I helped Mama by looking through all of the envelopes and carefully separating all of the pink ones (my favorite color) from the mess on the table. With a big smile, I presented her with the bills that I thought she should pay first. Fortunately, the pink envelopes served as notice of disconnect which needed Mama's urgent attention.

Mama did not have a car. She paid our bills in person; we walked to the rental office or around downtown Louisville to various office buildings. I seem to remember standing in long lines while handle our financial business. Mama would greet the ladies behind the desks with a smile. Then, she would open her crisp white envelops to remove some of her wrinkled green papers. With the green papers and pink envelopes in her hand, Mama would slide it all towards the ladies who would slowly count it. After the transaction was complete, I would then watch my mama walk away with pride. I knew that she was proud as evidenced by the squaring of her soft shoulders and with her head held high. I hustled to keep up with her spunky stride. I also felt a since of pride in knowing that I was able to help mama pay the pretty pink bills with the wrinkled green paper that had been first saved in the crisp white envelope.

Meanwhile, my mother began to be concerned about how I was holding up under the stress of single parenting. She had been the sole parent in our household for many years, caring for her disabled husband before he died. She had personal experience and knew that the load could be overwhelming. Mama acknowledged her concerns to me admitting that she worried that I was having a nervous breakdown. I told her that I was just fine not wanting to divulge the fact that I was having difficulty swallowing. During this period, the Surgeon General was broadcasting the ten danger signs of cancer and one of them being difficulty in swallowing. I had no money or health insurance, so I sought medical care from Louisville General Hospital that took welfare recipients as patients. Upon examination, the doctor's discovered that I had an overactive thyroid. I finally got an explanation of why I could eat so much and never gain so much as a pound. I gained only one pound in weight after each of my children's birth, which was really unheard of and unnatural. My doctor prescribed a plan of treatment that didn't involve surgery. I was instructed to take a little white pill each day for one year and undergo radiation once every quarter. It was an experimental program thought to have three major side effects; weight gain was a sure reality. I had to watch what foods I'd eat along with quantity from now on; hair loss was a maybe; and not being able to have children was a possibility. Becoming sterile was definitely not an issue, since I had five children already and didn't have any plans for more. The trial was successful with no sign of the overactive thyroid present at the end the year-long treatment.

I continued playing the piano and then the organ for my church services that brought in a few extra bucks. This arrangement was perfect since I enjoyed the fellowship and would be attending church regularly anyhow. It didn't pay much, but every little bit counted. Additionally, I worked outside of the home when I could doing "day work," which entailed cleaning another person's house for a small fee. It was on such occasion that I met a person who would help direct me to a future career.

NEW HOPE

Little did I know that when I stepped into her apartment on that Saturday morning that everything was about to change for the better. After answering an ad placed in the Louisville Courier-Journal newspaper for someone to do light cleaning for approximately 4 hours, I received a call from Ms. Connie Courteau offering me the job and I quickly accepted.

Upon arriving at her place in the east end of Louisville, I was greeted by a young woman about my age. She, too, seemed to be surprised at age. Ms. Courteau invited me to sit down so we could get acquainted. Working for Connie, as she asked me to call her, proved to be the easiest job I'd ever had. She seemed more interested in interviewing me than supervising my work.

Each Saturday when I arrived, I could smell bacon cooking and coffee brewing. We'd sat down to eat breakfast and she'd proceed picking my brain for details of my life's story. I soon figured out that she was intrigued by my intelligence and wanted to understand why I wasn't further along socially and financially than I was. Connie and I were the same age; she was white and I was black; we both had high hopes to succeed. So, what happened? Moreover, what could she do to help?

I told her my dreams of being a teacher from early childhood and how I would line up younger children on my front steps and pretend to teach them. However, upon graduating from high school without a scholarship available to me, I had to settle for business school. That fact perked her interest and she asked, "Have you heard about a training program that is available here in Louisville which is aimed to train and/or retrain people to reenter the work force?" When I told her that I had already inquired into that training and was told that there was approximately a year or two waiting list, she couldn't believe what she was hearing. Connie explained that just that week she had interviewed the supervisor of the program and was told they had place for some more applicants. Ms. Courteau moved quickly into action.

The next Monday, I got a call to come show up for class and I began studies on Tuesday. I will be forever grateful for that federally financed Manpower Development and Training Act (MDTA) that took a chance on me. I studied hard while *making excellent grades and successfully completed the training. As a result, I was offered an opportunity to teach the same remedial education that I had just completed. Do you know what that meant to me on all levels? First, it meant that I would be making more than three times the meager amount I received from Aid to Dependent Children. Still, more importantly, I had landed a responsible job (teaching), decent pay, and respect. I will forever be indebted to Connie Courteau who cared enough to act.*

Slowly but surely, I started moving up within the vocational school system, taking additional classes at University of Kentucky and Jefferson Community College. These classes were offered on site where I taught, and led into my getting employment at Jefferson Area Vocational School. My salary jumped from $450.00 a month to $800 plus. With the increase in salary came the notice to vacate our apartment in the housing projects. I didn't mind moving, but did not just want to go to another rental property. It was time to begin looking for our first home. We were all overjoyed.

The first order of business was to file and secure a divorce from Tommy. I was confident that there would be no trouble getting it, since he'd probably be happy to do so. Oh, what an exciting time! While I was thrilled by getting a house with a fence so I could have a garden, my children's excitement was centered on getting a dog who would need to be fenced.

We found the perfect home for us. It was a bungalow with two bedrooms and a full basement. Now, with added expenses of home ownership, I had to buckle down and continue on a tight budget. There was no place for laziness in mu household. Along with Debbie helping with the cooking, Keith and Glenn took care of our lawn which was much larger now. I invested in a gas lawn mower that was used to cut our grass and for the older boys to make extra money doing neighbors' yards. Del and Rodney were not excluded; they all had chores. Whenever the boys did outside work for other people like raking leaves, or shoveling snow, I could expect them to bring their earnings home and put it into the pot. In the meanwhile, I started investigating other ways to cut costs. One way I found was to learn to cut my boys' hair. This *Talk Story*, published in Troy State University's <u>Copper Blade Review</u>, 2003, tells the procedure and results of my efforts.

NEXT . . .

My personal finances were at an all-time low. I was struggling to provide for five children whose ages now ranged from eight to thirteen years. A friend of mine who was in the same predicament told me of a way in which she saved money and suggested that I learn to cut my boys' hair. I visualized how frugal this would be. Haircuts ran around five bucks each and I had three boys. So I invested in a small barbering kit with instructions, but soon found out that cutting hair was harder than it looked.

One day while I was watching television, I saw a commercial about a revolutionary gadget that was guaranteed to work or your money back. One that anyone could use safely and it only cost $2.95. It was described as a comb with a concealed razor. When you combed through the hair, it would trim the hair in a very simple manner leaving a well-groomed effect—and all this came with instructions.

So I rushed off to the nearest Walgreens Drug Store, purchased it, and called my sons to begin my barbering session. I called Keith first because he was the oldest, but he didn't want to go first. He remembered my last home-barbering adventure that left him completely bald right down the center of his head—giving him that reverse Mohawk look. So he said, "Thanks, but no thanks" and immediately disappeared. So I sent for Rodney, the youngest, but when he saw what I was about to do, he started crying for mercy. I would not be outdone, so I summoned Glenn, the middle son, who reluctantly agreed to let me experiment on him.

I read through the simple instruction one more time before making the first stroke. After I had tried several times without success, I began to think that I'd foolishly wasted my precious $2.95 on a worthless item. Just then I recalled reading that sometimes for longer hair, you would need to lower the razor blade a bit. So I did. Thinking that it would be better to start in the back of his head rather than the front or side, I began again. And presto…it cut! As I started to remove the loose hair, I was shocked to see that I had cut a segment of hair from the back of his neck that measured about one inch long and ½ inch wide leaving a big, slick spot at the base of his neck. The hair fell to the floor in one complete piece. For some reason, I picked up the hair and placed it on a piece of paper towel. It was late Saturday evening when my session began, so all of the barber shops were closed and I was in the worse fix ever.

To this day, I don't know what made me save that portion of cut hair intact, but I did. The next morning, being Sunday, we got up as usual and dressed for Sunday School. Though every time I looked at the back of Glenn's head and saw what I had done, I felt ill. Just then I got a great idea. I called for one of the kids to bring me the Elmer's School Glue. And …you guessed it! The hair glued back perfectly and I admonished Glenn not to be wiggling around during Sunday School and morning service. Glenn was about eleven at the *time and had never been known to sit still for any long period of time. He really did well that Sunday and had made it through Sunday School without a hitch. However, it was too good to last through the entire morning service.*

The devotional service was beginning, so my sister and I took our seats behind our children who were safely lined up in the pews in front of us. So, there we were--sitting in church trying to look as pious as we could—when my sister spotted something she thought was a bug crawling slowly down Glenn's neck. She swiped frantically at the insect when she discovered it was not a bug. It was hair! All that was left on Glenn's hairline was a white spot where the glue had been placed. She turned to look at me for an explanation, but by this time I was sick from trying to stifle my laughter. Why is it that things seem to be even funnier when you're in church?

Just a short time after settling into our new home, my sister, Julia, called to say she had a dog for us. Seems like a stray dog had come up on her porch and called us describing the dog as what sounded like a German shepherd. We hurried out to their house to claim our pet. When I saw what she thought to be a German shepherd, I knew I had been taken. There stood a skinny little dog that looked more like a cat than a dog. And there sister stood laughing and saying, "When I saw it, I thought it was a cat. You know I'm scared of cats. So I called Gartha and he picked it up and told me it was a dog. I called you because I knew your kids wanted a dog." I then asked what led her to think that this wimpy little dog with brown stripes was a German shepherd, and she laughed even harder. Meanwhile, my children had fallen in love with him and had named him *Butch*.

The rules of the household and the delegation of chores didn't change with a different address. I still expected everyone to pull his own weight, especially since I now was employed full time. They all were responsible for keeping their sleeping area clean and well as the common areas of the house. Both boys and girls took turn washing and/or drying dishes and cooking when old enough. I'll probably not live it down how I'd put Debbie in charge of seeing that tasks were completed. There is one example of how thorough she was in seeing that all I assigned was done. I'd like to share it with you.

WASTED

It was Wednesday evening and time for our weekly prayer meeting and choir rehearsals. I had instructed Debbie to make sure everybody was prepared to leave as soon as I came home from work.

The weather was hot that summer day in Louisville, so it made for a pleasant day to run and play outside. Debbie was outside with friends as were the rest, but when she saw it was time to stop playing and get ready for church, she called for her siblings to come in.

As usual, there was one unhappy camper...Glenn. He didn't object to going to church, but he hated to take a bath. However, he obeyed and subjected himself to soap and running water. They were cleaned up very nicely when I got home from work, and like they usually did, hugged and greeted me. All but Glenn.

"What's wrong, Glenn; don't you feel well?" I asked. He pouted his face up and rolled his eyes at Debbie and replied, "Debbie made us come in and get ready for church. I

answered, "So?" He continued, "And she made us take a bath!" Still puzzled, I said, "She did as I instructed." He then exclaimed loudly, "But what you don't know is that they cancelled choir rehearsal; (silence) she made me waste a bath for nothing!"

Overall, the next few years were uneventful and routine. But there are a few incidents and occurrences that I asked my five adult children to chime in on that stood out as memorable during the period when we were a family of six. These are their memories.

SWITCHED

Debby writes:

I was probably 10 years old, when one summer morning Mama stated, "All of you are getting spanked when I get home from work!" I don't remember what we did to deserve her attention but we were going to "get it". After searching through the 500+ paged cookbook to find a recipe to prepare for dinner with the meager staples we had on hand, I developed a plan to stop Mama from acting on her promise. I gathered all of my younger siblings and shared the strategy. Since it was Mama's custom of sending us outside to extract our own switch (a green slim tree branch stripped of most of its leaves), we would dispose the neighborhood of all lower branches before she got home. I made a simple tuna noodle casserole and put it on the back of the four-burner gas stove before baking it. We then collected our tools (all of the scissors and knives we could find in the apartment) and carried all of the plastic covered kitchen chairs with their heavy metal silver frames outside under the trees. Under the blazing summer sun, Keith, Glenn and I stood in the sturdy chairs on our tippy-toes to cut and pull down all of the branches with the potential to become switches. Del and Rodney had the task of piling up all of the trimmings. Tree by tree, we became self-proclaimed arborists. Soon, our friends joined us in our protest effort. Before long, the neighborhood children had removed all of the switches in that block and took them to what we called the incinerator (a dumpster area for trash cans). Exhausted… my siblings and I took a nap.

Mama's arrival was greeted with the smell of my baked casserole filled with canned fish and crusty cheese along with hugs and kisses from five scheming children. She was excited to see us, too. She took a nice, long, warm bath. We thought, surely, she forgot about that promise. She ate dinner with us, asked us about our day and listened to our generic stories while I tried to keep Del and Rodney from spilling the beans about what we really did. Mama told us that she was tired from a hard day at work but she was not too tired to spank our butts. We knew what she would tell us to next, "Somebody, go outside and get me a good switch!"

Since all of us felt that her request was directed at us individually, we collectively walked slowly down those dark yet polished concrete stairs outside to collect the "uncollectible". We must have been gone for a while because she opened the window to call for us in the order of our birth, "Debbie, Keith, Glenn, Del and Rodney: Get in here!" We ran back up the steps in record time, huffing and puffing and claiming our inability to find any switches. Mama said, "That's okay, I will get my own switch." And she hustled down those steps as we ran to peer out the kitchen window. We tried to hold it inside but could not resist from giggling at her reaching for what she could not touch. By the time Mama *searched for green slim branched suitable for switching at the second tree, we were rolling in laughter and wondered if she could hear us. A nosy on-looking neighbor with no children hollered at Mama through her window and spilled the beans, "Your children cut down all of the switches earlier today and their friends helped them". Mama turned around on a dime and headed back into the apartment. We heard her coming back up those steps with a heavy thud. Some of us were still laughing and some had tears in their eyes with nervous anticipation. We were surprised to see her face; Mama switched. She was smiling and broke out in laughter at the sight of us huddled together at the kitchen window. On this day, Mama stretched out her loving and compassionate arms to us and we ran forward to receive her love.*

STORIES FROM THE PAST

Keith writes:

These are a few of the incidents I remember from our life in Beecher Terrace, Louisville, KY, during the early 60s. Most of these occurred between 1962 and 1966.

Residents of Beecher Terrace attended the Taylor Elementary School. It was a nice school in hindsight, but at the time I hated it. I started school as a five year old since my birthday was in December. While in the first grade I had a crush on my teacher and would not miss school so I could be in her class. Near the end of the school year she missed several days of school and eventually we were told that she had died. I intentionally left her name off since the details could be considered sensitive in nature. The second grade was much different and may have been the reason I hated school. I thought my teacher had to make my life miserable everyday which usually resulted in me getting paddled by her or the Principal for something I did or refused to do. In those days parents were told when their child was spanked. That meant I could expect a second spanking when I got home. So as a six year old genius, I devised a plan that would stop all of the daily torture I was receiving. I knew I would not be sent to school sick, so I faked an illness that was hard to detect. My sickness was an upset stomach. I may have gotten away with it once but after knowing that the solution was castor oil. Can anybody say "Healed"? My next plan was to misplace one shoe. That didn't work long either. Somehow, I made it through the year and was looking forward to going to the third grade. Since I had missed several days of school, I also failed several subjects and had to repeat the second grade. The next year I thought my experience would be different with a different teacher. Boy, was I wrong, I got the same teacher.

A few years later, my brothers and I were old enough to do some chores for some neighbor's like raking leaves and taking the trash cans to the street. In the winter we would shovel snow and cut grass in the summer with a manual push mower. The money we earned was used to buy things we wanted and Mom could not get us since she was always busy taking care of us and making sure we had the things we needed. Even at a young age we had learned the importance of taking care of family. We watched out for each other and for Mom. I don't remember when we started doing this but at some point we started to give Mom some of the money we earned to help with bills. I believe it helped ease some of the burden of raising five children alone and I praise God for *blessing us with a mom that sacrificed so much to make sure we grew up in safety and love.*

Our grandmother and aunt also lived in Beecher Terrace in another building across a court which seemed very large but was actually a small park. Every Saturday my sister Debbie would go to their apartment to spend the night. Saturday night, Debbie came home after being tripped by a group of boys that had tied a rope between two fence posts to trip people walking between the buildings. Our mom and I went with Debbie to escort her back to Grandma's apartment. Mom took a pair of scissors with us and we got to the spot, she cut the rope and told the boys to stop hurting people trying to pass that area and to go home. Mom then told me to go back to our apartment and stay with my siblings. She took Debbie to Grandma's apartment as planned. As we walked away, I heard the boys talking among themselves. Since I could not tell what they were saying, I hid behind some bushes and watched them. In those days, when an adult told us to do something, we did it. Those boys stayed at the spot and tied the rope back together and hid waiting for Mom to walk by. I knew they were up to no good so I stayed hidden and watched them until Mom got close to the spot. Just before she got close enough to trip, I jumped out and warned her of the rope and where the boys were hiding. This time Mom cut the rope up into so many small pieces that it would be impossible for them to put it back together. After that event, we continued to walk Debbie to Grandma's apartment but we never saw those boys again.

I LOVE ANIMALS

Glenn writes:

I've always been fascinated with animals. Anything that moved or crawled, I wanted. The housing projects we lived in didn't allow pets such as dogs and cats, so I turned my attention to lizards, mice, snakes and other creepy crawly things. I really wanted a dog, but we weren't allowed to have one in the housing project. Mama did let us have a hamster that we enjoyed until he got loose from his cage and started gnawing on things. We knew his days were numbered after he ate holes in Mama's sweet potatoes.

A friend of Mama's gave us a guinea pig. It was so cute with its white, beige, and brown colored hair that was long and fluffy. It didn't look nothing like the hamster; it was bigger. We had a meeting to decide on its name. Everybody except me was suggesting male names. I tried to tell them that the guinea pig was a girl but they didn't believe me. I was out voted so they chose to name it "Tommy" which was our missing father's name.

One day when I had Tommy out of the cage playing with him on the couch, Keith and I began wrestling and Keith landed on him. Tommy squealed loudly and then started whistling. I knew then he was hurt badly. Everybody started running toward the couch, when suddenly we noticed that six little bags had come out of our pet. I screamed, "I told you it was a girl!" So right on the spot we changed its name from Tommy to Tammy. Meanwhile, Mama picked up the babies and proceeded to take them to the incinerator. By this time I was crying, "But Mama they're not dead." Mama thought they were and everybody agreed with her. Once again I was *overruled. I watched as Mama put them in a bag and carried them to our garbage station and threw them away.*

A couple of days later, we could hear her baby guinea pigs whistling just like Tammy. It was a miracle they had lived, but there they were walking around the neighborhood. Her offspring were adopted and raised by some of my friends. Later that day, we noticed Tammy limping and took her to a veterinarian. This particular Vet had been recently featured on the local news as one who worked on all sorts of strange exotic animals—those nobody else would touch. Mama thought it was worth a try so she called him and explained our plight. He agreed to examine Tammy. It was the first guinea pig he'd ever treated. Tammy's leg was fractured. The doctor put a splint on it and sent her home with us. Tammy lived about ten more years. We really enjoyed waking up every morning to her lurid whistle.

I GOT YOUR BACK

Delphia writes:

There is an important lesson I learned as a child that is still true today. I know that I can always count on my brothers and sisters. We were like any other group of siblings. With Mom working long hours, Aunt Maxie and Grandma were around to keep an eye on us. But we spent a lot of time alone, so you can imagine we fought a lot. But more importantly we had each other's back.

Mom didn't have the time to personally clean the house. So, she assigned each of us a room that we were responsible for: the living room, kitchen, bathroom, den, etc. Chore assignments rotated every week. If Mom came home and there was something out of place in the living room, she didn't ask who did it. She went to the party responsible for that room.

One example of this stands out in my mind. I always wanted to be with the popular kids. I remember some new girls moved in the neighborhood when we lived on Greg Avenue. I knew they would be instantly popular, so to get the inside friendship track I spent as much time as I could with them. The previous Christmas the boys, Keith, Glenn, and Rodney all got bikes. Those girls didn't have any. They convinced me to "borrow" my brothers' bikes so we could take a ride. I knew two things. My brothers would never agree to let me use their bikes, and Debby, who was always in charge, would totally forbid me from going anywhere! I made my own decision to take the bikes and go.

I had no idea that these girls were leading me to the worst housing projects in Louisville…Southwick! If I knew that, I probably wouldn't have gone. I was scared the whole time. But I had to play it off like I was cool. But in my mind, I thought about how dangerous that place was. Then it hit me! I didn't do my chores! As time got later and later I had two reasons to be afraid. The basic danger of the place but even more terrifying was Mom getting home and my assigned room would not be clean.

To my surprise, when I got home, my siblings were happy that I was home safe. And best of all, they took care of my chores. I know that whatever I am going through or in need of, my siblings have my back! The icing on the cake is, back then there were five of us. God blessed me with another brother and sister that have the same frame of mind. They have my back and they know I have theirs!

Over time, our family didn't seem to be as broken as I felt it had. We had settled down into a routine where rules of order and discipline had been established. In hindsight, I now see that it was a time when I was the most vulnerable. Then I let my guard down and the old enemy leaped in to do what he does best.

LIFE DISJOINTED

It would prove to be the most turbulent time I would ever experience, although, it seemed like an innocent encounter the night I met Edward. I had boarded a bus in downtown Louisville to go to Newburg, a suburb area of the city, where Julia and her family resided. My sister was very involved with the Elks organization and her lodge was having a Friday night fish fry to raise money. A reliable person was seeing after my kids who were about seven to twelve years of age by now. I had no other plans for the night but to have fun with family and friends.

Edward got on the bus a few blocks away from where I boarded, spotted me, and asked politely if I minded him sitting next to me. How could I refuse such a courteous offer? I said, "No." And that short two-lettered word began a friendly conversation. I discovered that he and my sister knew each other from high school. In fact, they were in the same class, although they hadn't seen each other for years. I called Julia to verify his statement and she exclaimed, "Yes, I know Edward. Invite him out to the fish fry?" When we arrived, Edward appeared to know everybody there; he was in his old neighborhood. We exchanged telephone numbers and got even more knowledgeable of each other. After a few weeks, we became more than friends. Looking back now, I can see that it was a combination of loneliness and just plain physical desire that led me into further involvement with him. I was about thirty-five years old. However, I didn't enter the relationship blindly. I asked all the "right" questions and he dutifully gave me all the answers I wanted to hear. I found out that he had a meager job making minimum wage. That didn't concern me. How could it since it hadn't been that long ago

67

that I was on welfare? On the other hand, I expected him to be truthful about matters of faith. He told me that he was a Christian but had not been attending church regularly which again seemed to be a reasonable explanation. Soon Edward began attending church with me and my children and eventually joined the fellowship as well as the choir. It pleased me that he was good to my children and that they all liked him. Then everything changed.

He began questioning my every move. His jealousy began to hinder my relationship with my family as well as with that of long-time friends. Someone once said, "Jealousy fused with paranoia can be a toxic combination." He evidently felt threatened by my teaching position and my popularity and began to believe that I would quit seeing him.

At first, Edward didn't mind my association with fellow employees as long as they were females. That too changed and it began to affect how I would come and go. I hated being suspected of cheating on him on my every move, no matter whether it was at church or work. So, I confronted him about his jealousy and he promised he would change. But, of course, he didn't. In addition, he knew I had found out things about his past that he was trying to keep hidden. He had been in prison on two separate occasions and had served time for felony crimes. So after he knew these facts became known to me, he'd tell me that he had nothing to lose. If he committed another crime, he would get life in prison on the "three strikes, you're out" law. So things got worse and escalated into to physical assault. I will never forget the fear that gripped me every time he'd say, "If I can't have you, nobody else will. I'll kill you and all your children" I admit I was afraid of him and his threats to harm me and my children. Nonetheless, I knew I couldn't go on living in fear forever. That was it! I had never had a man strike me before and I wasn't going to start now. I *had reached the point where I'd had enough. It was time for me to make a stand against him, so I told him it was over.*

I began to confess my transgressions to the Lord reflecting on 'how in the world I ended up in such a quagmire'. Having been reared so differently and having accepted Jesus as my Savior, I asked, "How could I have been so blind?" I remember praying this exact prayer, "Lord, please forgive me. You alone know me and have shown me that you have a plan for my life and for the precious lives of my children. Restore me to a right relationship with you. And if I'm to ever have a mate, I will wait patiently for you to provide. You know I'm stubborn and hard-headed, so when you speak to me, please make it plain. Amen."

One day I went into the Principal's office to inquire of a school matter and there in his office set the best-looking man I'd ever laid eyes on. I recall his attire very vividly. He had on a dark suit, striped tie and had a pipe dangling loosely from his mouth. Then I heard the Lord plainly speak (as I'd prayed He would do), "That's him." And I replied, "You didn't do badly, Lord!" Excitedly, I left the principal's office and went into the secretary's office and I asked, "Who is that fine man? Is he interviewing for a teaching job here? Pull his file for me." The name on the application was "Willard Hunt". It was June 1968, and he had recently retired from the United States Army after 20 years of service. Everything in his file was looking good, but my jubilance diminished after seeing a big "M" in the marital status section. Well, I thought to myself, *"The Lord owed me an explanation about this one; I know He wouldn't hook me up with a married man."*

Confused beyond words, I left her office and began a strategy aiming to defend the feelings I had immediately developed for this stranger. He was hired as an automobile mechanic instructor in the shop section, but was frequently in and out of the main building where I worked. I was courteous enough to him, I guess, but somewhat standoffish. As I observed his interaction with others, I concluded that he thought more highly of himself as he ought; therefore, I rejected any good gesture offered me. Such as the times when our monthly pay would be held up due to an error on payroll. When this happened, no one would get paid until it was corrected. We relied on our checks coming on time, especially since we had waited all month. Meanwhile, there was this Mr. Hunt coming to the aid of anyone needing a loan. When, he approached me with the offer, I turned him down. I know he knew something about my family life by now, but I was too proud to ask. I'd refuse his offer over and over again until one situation arose when our paychecks were sent back to be redone because of a penny mistake. That's the straw that broke the camel's back, so to speak. I had no choice but to swallow my pride and ask. I had pegged him to be arrogant and bigheaded. He demonstrated the opposite. Mr. Hunt reached for his billfold and asked how much I needed to carry me over until payday, adding that if I needed more to simply ask.

For several months, we continued to treat each other cordially whenever we were in each other's presence. Mr. Weismann, the coordinator of Jefferson Area Vocational School, had gotten authorization to begin yet another training school in Louisville and promoted me to Coordinator of the Salisbury School. It was another boost for my career and I knew when Edward found out it would add to his low self-esteem and jealousy. Never the less, I gladly accepted the challenge that lay ahead of me. Salisbury students were chosen from a pool of unemployed and/or under-employed people ranging from 18-21 years of age who showed interest in being trained to increase the probability for higher wages and advancement. I was especially qualified for the coordinator position because I could relate on many levels to all the students. Most notably to those women who were recipients of ADC (Aid to Dependent Children) like I had been. The new training would entail completion of a 6-week assessment of the students' overall interest in retraining. This was accomplished by allowing each student to rotate bi-weekly through three courses of their choice. After which, they would be placed into a longer course of training matching their abilities and skills. Planned careers for Salisbury students included clerk typists, dental assistants, counter girls, surgical assistants and more. Meanwhile, Hunt's (I'd dropped the "mister" by now and was simply addressing him by his last name) place of employment was broadening opportunities for employment also for its students by offering more choices such as carpentry, brick-laying, and electrical training. They were still keeping their former courses: auto mechanics, auto body, and welding.

Because of our positions of School Coordinators, we became assigned to shop together for supplies needed for both schools. I knew what training materials the Salisbury school would need and Hunt had knowledge of the necessary shop supplies. This was a daunting task because Hunt and I had to spend millions of government money to get these programs up and running. Personally, I was not thrilled with the fact of being in his presence for hours upon hours each day and I think the feeling was mutual. But we diligently thrust ourselves into the task ahead, just talking only when it was necessary.

Two days had passed without any conversation that wasn't a necessity when he spoke up and asked, "What have I done to you to make you so unfriendly toward me? I

71

understand you are friendly and talkative to others, so it must be me." I definitely didn't expect such a bluntly asked question, but there it was. Bam! It was right out there nice and clear and there was nothing I could do but search for an answer. I finally answered, "It is not you; I'm just going through a little something, that's all. He said, "I know what you mean. We all go through tough times now and then. Do you want to share? After all, looks as if we'll be stuck together for the next week or two." And then he said, "I'll go first." Hunt went on to explain that his marriage has fallen apart and that he had been locked out of his home. He was temporarily living in the shop and sleeping on his desk. Boy, was that a shocker! He surely didn't appear to be someone *homeless,* but of course, one never knows what another person is going through.

I could relate to his pain and was finally ready to open up to him. He told me more personal details and I listened carefully. He said, "As you know, I've just recently retired from the army and am presently married. This is my second marriage; the first one happened when I was not quite twenty years old. That marriage only lasted about eight months and ended in annulment. It appears that she married me to be her meal ticket which was a common practice for women wanting the financial security of being a military wife. So, a rocky start ended abruptly with her being arrested and incarcerated for attempting to murder me. After that fiasco, I planned to be very cautious from then on and not fall in love so quickly. I met my present wife, Margaret, when I was in my mid-twenties, and a young soldier stationed at Fort Knox. She was somewhat older than I was (about fourteen years older to be exact) and had four teenaged children, but that didn't matter to me. I loved children and I had always been attracted to older women. We got married and everything appeared to be okay, at least it seemed to be okay each time I returned home from overseas assignments and such. However, every time the subject of having a family came up, I was shut down immediately. She would say that she didn't want to *mix her children*. I still don't understand what that meant. Having a child with me would somehow mix her children? Even so, we managed to stay hitched. Over my entire army career, I only came home on leave a few weeks at a time, even though I was allowed a thirty-day leave each year. I did so in order to save the money I would use traveling back and forth to provide for my family. Over time, we had an empty nest and I was able to send even more money back home expecting Margaret to faithfully manage it. After completing my 20-year tour, and to my dismay, our bank account was empty. I forgave her mishandling of funds after she offered a somewhat lame excuse that all revolved around her continual support of her grown children. It didn't take long for me to realize that I had been used. Our relationship was 'great' as long as I was away, but after I returned to the States, she turned cold. Ultimately, she began to withdraw her affections and we started sleeping apart. If fact, we didn't do anything together. She'd prepare my food, set it on the table, and go into another room leaving me to eat alone. We had a large spacious home with plenty of rooms so I chose to sleep in one of the upstairs bedrooms.

The next week, one of my co-workers asked to borrow my truck to move someone and I agreed. He took my truck and put me out at home. It was early afternoon and I went upstairs to my room to nap when I heard voices downstairs. I quietly opened my door and went down to the landing to hear what was being said. To my surprise, there sat my wife with her sister openly plotting a plan to kill me. I thought privately, "Oh Lord, not again!"

I had heard enough. I slipped back into my room and didn't come out quietly this time. When I approached, my wife innocently spoke saying, "Oh, I didn't know you were home. Where is your truck?" I replied, "I lent it out." I stayed at the house knowing I had no place to go, at least until I asked permission to temporarily stay in the shop until I acquired an apartment. She must have become suspicious because a couple of days after that incident, she filed for divorce, had the locks changed to the house, and sent me the bill. I will soon be moving into my own place."

I could have cuddled Hunt right up at that moment and just held him tight, but I restrained myself. However, I saw clearly that he was to be my confidant. There was no one else, even among family and friends that I felt comfortable confiding in apart from him. I pondered to myself: *Is this what the Lord meant when He said, "that's him"? Of course, it is. Here is my soul mate; the one the Lord had prepared for me and neither of us had been willing to wait for God's timing. Consequently, our getting ahead of God's plan had caused us both much heartache.*

The next day, I began pouring my heart out to him and it was the best decision I had made, at least in a long time. I explained, "I have gotten myself into a real mess. I met this guy a couple of years ago and he seemed nice at the time. Then he showed a jealous which has escalated into physical violence and threats. I think he feels like I'm too good for him, and recently I have begun to feel the same. He has committed serious felony crimes and served time in prison. I didn't know this until much later into our relationship. Now, since I've broken up with him, he has gotten worse. I feel trapped and I'm living under constant threats of harm to me and my kids." Hunt then asked, "Has he ever verbally threatened you with bodily harm?" I replied, "He has." And he firmly said, "You are in imminent danger. I've been all over the world and have witnessed a lot of things. Every time I've become aware of a situation like this, I found that it doesn't pay to ignore it. Some people will tell you to not worry because he doesn't mean what he is saying, but I won't. It's been my experience that when a man tells a woman, *'if I can't have you nobody else will'*, he means business." I then asked, "What should I do?" Little did I know I was about to receive some invaluable information from him. He answered, "I'll tell you what you should to protect your family. First you must arm yourself." To which I replied, "You mean get a gun? I have never held a gun no less shot one. I wouldn't know what to do with one if I had it." He retorted, "I'll show you," and continued, "Secondly, you must contact the police and get a restraining order against him which will prevent him from coming within so many yards of you and your home."

That afternoon, he took me to a pawn shop, purchased a 38-caliber gun, and he showed me how to use it. His instruction was simple and straightforward. He said, "Just point and shoot." I followed his instruction exactly and in addition made my neighbors aware of Edward's threats so they could be on the lookout, too. I told my children to not let him approach them at any time and that we were not friends anymore. The gun was put in a safe place within my reach and was fully loaded. I felt I had done everything I could do to protect us, but still I knew he was watching my every move.

CRISIS

It was about two o'clock in the morning when I heard a hard knock at my door. There it was again. I leaped from my bed and called out, "Who is it?" Fear gripped me as Edward identified himself and asked me to open the door pleading that he just wanted to talk. I yelled, "No! Get away from my door! " I did have the presence of mind to grab the gun from its hiding place. I reached for the telephone to call the police when suddenly, without any further warning, he burst through the front door, broke it down, and there he stood, right in full view with a gun in hand.

Our house was a small bungalow with two bedrooms and a basement. The girls slept in the front bedroom, I slept in the back one, and the boys slept in the basement. The front door entered into the living room area which joined a kitchen that emptied into the hallway. I had an open floor plan way before it became in vogue.

Motivated by fear, I did the only thing I could do at the time. Shoot? No. I ran! I took off running into the kitchen to the living room and back through the hallway. While I was running, Edward was trying to get a good shot off. He fired his weapon and missed. I continued trying to allude him when he fired again. Two shots were expended. I sensed I was in a trance or something similar to it, when a loud command ran out. It resonated from the girl's room and it was the voice of my oldest daughter, Debbie. Her voice pierced through all the chaos going on with clear instructions… "Shoot, Mama, shoot!"

I fired one shot and that was all that was needed to drop his body to the floor. Have you ever experienced God's providential care and protection surrounding you, shielding you from harm? I did that night. Edward was so close to me, no more than seven or eight feet away at any time. How come he could miss hitting me? I know it was the Lord.

Police arrived almost immediately afterwards. Evidently, my neighbors had made the call to them. The officers came in and asked me a few questions and were *starting to leave when one of the officers spoke. He said, "I know you have to cry right now, but keep your spirits up and count your blessings. I have responded to many domestic violence situations like this and I only wished other restraining orders would end this way with the victim surviving."*

It took a while for me to get over the tragic events of that October night, but with help from my pastor, a loving family, and many loyal friends, I did. Hunt was being especially helpful and supportive. When summoned, he came quickly to my aid. He met my family for the first time that night and was well received by all. I knew he was special and he exhibited it by comforting my children insuring them that they were safe now. Moreover, he handily repaired the broken door so that we could finally get some much needed sleep. Of course, sleep was not in the cards for me that night. To this day, I count the anniversary of that night in October, 1969 as another birthday, symbolizing when my life was spared along with a new spiritual dedication. October of 1969 also denoted the beginning of a long, beautiful love affair that had already begun to blossom.

By the time the Thanksgiving holiday came around, we were hooked by "lock, stock, and barrel", so to say. We had both experienced unimaginable heartbreak and deception. I introduced Hunt to everybody I cared about. My children thought he was great and Debby, then fifteen, really liked his blue Volkswagen. Then, we decided to go to his hometown, Tulsa, Oklahoma to meet his side of the family, and to especially meet his mother. And true to form, the apple didn't fall too far from the tree. Mother Pauline was a saintly widow who conveyed her approval of me right away. My mother would always tell me that she could tell what kind of person someone was after meeting his mother. I thought to myself,

"Wow! I've become my mother." I must admit that meeting her erased all doubts about the character of the man I'd fallen hard for. After returning home, encouraged by a positive visit, we thrust ourselves into the *get-to-know-you* better mode.

How can I best describe him? I've already said that he was very good looking. Several people would comment on how much he favored the late Dr. M. L. King Jr. and I agreed.

Ironically enough, their birthdays were close, too: Hunt's birthday on Jan. 12, 1930 and King's on Jan. 15, 1929. His family were poor sharecroppers. In fact, he had made his decision to join the army due to a very bleak financial return on a whole year's work. He told me that his family had worked the entire year sharecropping and only netted 100 dollars. He was not quite eighteen when a friend of his told him of his plans to enlist and asked him to join with him on a "Buddy Program". He said, "Why not? There's gotta be something out there better than this." Hunt was honorably discharged from the military after serving twenty years. High on the list of his accomplishments was an incident where Chinese soldiers surrendered to him. Young and scared to death, he followed the correct protocol and received merits for his actions. Then when President Truman signed the order to end segregation throughout the military, he was chosen to be among the first groups to do so. Hunt admitted that volunteering for the U. S. Army was the best decision he had made thus far. Years later he would make an even greater one…to accept Jesus as his Lord and Savior. His mother had told him that when the Lord touched him, he would know. Every time he told the story of his conversion, he'd say, "I went to church that Sunday morning mad and came out glad." But he confessed, he got disgruntled with church membership while listening to all the gossip flowing from his ex-wife's lips each Sunday after worship service. Being fed up with the hypocrisy, he stopped attending church on a regular basis.

Getting to know Hunt better was my topmost mission. I admit I was attracted by his generosity. It appeared that he really did have money and didn't mind spending it. I was getting spoiled at record speed. It was my first time dining at some of Louisville's best and most expensive restaurants. It was also the first time I had eaten a *real* steak or washed one down with a glass of expensive wine. Thinking back on those times, I believe knowing I finally met a gentleman willing and ready to treat me so special, opened my heart in a way I had never felt before. I remember thinking out loud, "If this is what true love is, I want it".

The days of chivalry had returned, at least they had for me. What I had to learn was to step back and permit him to open my door, pull my chair out, and simply let him treat me like a lady. This was definitely new territory I was entering, but my mother didn't raise any fools. I became a quick study.

I also learned that he loved to cook but had never gotten the time to experiment. My children and I were more than happy to be his guinea pigs. Whatever meal he prepared was always that of choice meat for which he barred no expense. Hunt didn't move into our home, but the barbecue grill his students made for him out of a 50-gallon drum, did. I still have it. That was over fifty years ago. It's been painted many times to retard rusting. I recall the first time he came to show off his grilling skills. It was on an unusually warm November day. I was expecting him to prepare the usual picnic items like hamburgers or hot dogs, but out of the cellophane wrapping came boneless ribeye steaks…enough for everybody. I'm stressing the point that it was everybody, because former friends would have had hot dogs/hamburgers for the kids, and steaks for us. But not this man, he had steaks for all of us. I knew then that he wasn't the sort of person who would make a difference between kids either. Duly noted!

We settled into a wonderful relationship, but it wasn't without scrutiny. Oh yes, our family had their goggles of us and on me in particular. And rightfully so. I didn't have good track record with men in the past, so how could they reasonably expect anything different? They thought they were working undercover, but we had them figured out. It seemed that my brother, Buckle, was the chief investigator, while Mama and his twin sister, Maxie were the supervisors. Whenever Buckle showed up expectantly, he was always made to feel welcome and was assured that he could drop by anytime. Sometimes he'd find Hunt repairing something broken, helping with lawn maintenance, or simply just relaxing. But we never gave him negative ammunition to take back. Well, it was this one time that came close. We were all in the basement where the boys slept and Hunt was replacing a part from my washer. Buckle had come on downstairs and as usual, he and Hunt greeted each other with a handshake. That's when he saw what he thought was a wedding ring and inquired about it. Glenn overheard the conversation and popped in saying, "That's his high school ring!" All was well.

By Christmas that year, Hunt learned a few more significant tidbits about me and my family traditions. We both came from poor hardworking families but evidently had diverse ways of celebrating Christmas. His family didn't put much importance on the holiday when it came to gift giving. And mine did, even if they were home-made, we gave each other a gift. Moreover, he believed that if someone needed shoes, why not buy them now; I wanted to wait until Christmas so it would be one of the gifts. So we agreed to disagree for then anyway, and the two of us went shopping. Hunt was quiet and attentively observing each item I'd put in the cart. I had clothes and games for Debby; a doll and tea set for Del; trucks and action figures for Rodney. But when I picked a toy tool set, he asked, "Now, who is this for?" I said, "Glenn." He replied, "How old is Glenn? I thought he was about twelve. Am I right?" When I answered, "Yes." Hunt said, "That's it. I've seen enough." From then on, I just stood back and observed while he loaded my shopping cart with *real* saws, hammers, vices, along with nails, screws and everything an apprentice carpenter would need. I said to myself, "That's all good, but who's going to pay for all this stuff, and of equal importance, how would it all fit under the tree?" I tried to not think about Glenn's gifts, since I still had not secured Keith's gift. I knew what he wanted, because he was aspiring to be a scientist someday. I proceeded to the toy department with Hunt following close by. There were only a few telescopes available to choose from that were within my budget. As I pondered my dilemma, Hunt said, "And this is what you're looking to buy for Keith who's fourteen?" He then immediately turned, walked to the checkout, and paid for every item in the basket, while I stood with my mouth wide open...speechless. You guessed it. After that I followed his lead. Next, we went to a large store that sold all kinds of sporting equipment and he found what he was searching—a top of the line telescope. Two hundred dollars was peeled off of his seeming inexhaustible stack of bills. Overall, we both got an education. He learned that he'd have to let me do some of the traditional activities I was used to doing. I learned that he was more generous than I, when it came to spending. He proved to me that he wasn't stingy one bit. I showed him that I wanted to get the most value out of each purchase. The primary lesson I got from our shopping trip was this—I needed someone of his stature in my life to be there for me and my children. Then I praised God that I found him.

January brought in cold and snowy weather along with a visit from the "supervisors" as I called them. They had all the information they needed to make a final sweep. It was about dinner time when Hunt peered out the front window and announced, "I think you have visitors coming." I knew I hadn't invited anybody over. I looked out the front window and let out a loud gasp, "It's my mother and sister!" After taking another glance. He said, "Oh, two ducks." I replied, "What do you mean by describing them as "two ducks?" He answered, "What else can you call them? They're short, fat, and waddle when they walk." I had to laugh but couldn't let them hear me. They entered and were introduced to my new and dear friend. (Remember Hunt was an Oklahoma farm boy.) I said, "Mother, this is Willard Hunt." And to Hunt, I said, "Hunt, this is my mother, Cordie Guthrie." Then show time began…Hunt bent half way down, grabbed her hand, and graciously said, "How do you do, Ma'am?" Mama was won over immediately, smiling with a slight giggle. I noticed Maxie was also impressed by his manners as I introduced her next. The children all ran into the living room to greet their auntie and grandma with hugs and kisses. Maxie noticed the smell of something baking coming from the kitchen. Debbie announced, "I'm making Mr. Hunt a cake. It's his birthday!" The rest of the evening went extremely well. Hunt was forthcoming and honest in his answers to their inquiries. Maxie was amazed by his intelligence. They stayed for dinner topped off with birthday cake and ice cream. Soon he would meet the rest of my clan.

The court date for Hunt's divorce was looming in the next weeks and he was anxiously waiting for the results. He was confident that he had done everything he could to keep the marriage together. I had no problem believing it to be so based on what I now knew about his character. It turned out that he had been worrying in vain. She wanted the house, furniture, and $300 per week alimony. She got all the furniture and $125 a month for one year and was not a happy camper. The judge ruled in his favor giving him the house and his freedom. However, she didn't leave the premises without leaving her mark. When Hunt took me to see the house for the first time, I was impressed by its size and beauty. The neighborhood was upscale, too, with a golf club a couple blocks away and a city park within walking distance. I filed all this in the back of my mind…for later. It was March and the weather was a little chilly, but not cold enough for use of utilities. Then I saw the rice. Yes, rice! It was everywhere…on the carpet, in the window sills, in the kitchen cabinets and any other place you can imagine. Still, that childish prank didn't affect the charm of the house. However, as I looked on I felt uneasy being in the home that he'd shared with another woman.

Over the years, folk, have asked us what events actually led to our finalizing plans to get married. The honest answer is neither one of us could recall. I said that Hunt asked me to marry him; he claimed he didn't and that I popped the question. All I know is that we knew it would be and so did everyone else. I never had any doubts that Willard Hunt was the man God had for me. But, that it seemed God's plan for us was birthed before he ever met me. It was as if Hunt knew he'd have a large family someday. First, he ordered a brand new station wagon upon departing Germany for home in 1968. He picked his new car up in Detroit. Then he purchased a four bedroom house that was larger than two people needed. Was this just a coincidence? I don't think so. I think it was God quietly moving in our lives unbeknownst to us. Yes. You'd probably agree with me that it's a good thing He chooses to do it this way. Lord knows that if we got our hands on His plans, we'd surely mess them up.

One morning, I felt it was time to share our marriage plans with my children. When I did, cheers broke out in the room. I heard a series of questions coming from the group, such as, "Can I call him Dad?" was the most popular one. "When? Is he going to live with us?" I was thrilled that they all approved so fully, but I noticed that I hadn't heard my oldest child say anything. Puzzled, I turned to see tears welding up in my 15- year-old's eyes. I must admit that I was shocked at her questions. She asked, "Why do you have to get married? Why don't you just live together?" I patiently explained that when a man and woman love each other, they want to seal their love under the umbrella of marriage as God has ordained. Debby appeared to understand my defense, but that didn't lessen her worry. She was afraid of losing her place in my heart. After all she had been my loving daughter and my confidant. Also concerning her was all the stories she had heard about what step-fathers do to girls and she desperately wanted to protect her little sister. I knew she'd be watching his every move. Lastly and maybe most important was that she had personally witnessed the assault Edward made on me and feared that it would be repeated. It was a lot for a teenage girl to comprehend. Then I hugged her tightly and promised her that I, along with the entire family, would be okay.

On June 17th, Hunt got the call from his lawyer that his divorce was final. Excitedly, he called me to meet him at his attorney's office. It was about two o'clock on a Wednesday afternoon. We met there thinking it wouldn't take long to sign a few papers, but little did we know, his lawyer had other things on his mind. It seems he was expecting Hunt to come alone. Finally, as we left his office, he whispered to Hunt, "Next time, come by yourself." That became a standing joke between us from then on. He knew a good man when he saw one! But now, we had more important things to take care of like applying for a marriage license. My niece, Connie, was getting married on that coming Saturday, June 20th, and if things worked out, we had gotten her permission to have a *double ceremony*. Well, it wouldn't be really a double one. Our ceremony would follow theirs. Everything was ready: the venue-my sister's home: the preacher: our pastor, the guests: our family and friends. However, we definitely had to apply for the license that day…three days before wedding and really had to hurry now. The clock was reading 3:00 p.m. The marriage license office closed at 4:00 p.m. which ordinarily wouldn't be a big deal, but…

My future husband was not the swiftest man on foot. Usually, he just took his time getting from one place to another, not so today! He drove over ten city blocks in Louisville's rush-hour traffic, dropped me off in front of the building, parked four blocks away, and ran back to make it to the 5th floor probate office with five minutes to spare. I was both amazed and happy that he made it before closing. The wedding date was set—Saturday, June 20, 1970 at 4:00 p.m. I only had two days to make my wedding dress.

Part III

MY MARRIAGE TO WILLARD

I left early that morning in order to get to my sister's home and dress before guests were scheduled to arrive. And I, of course, left Debby in charge to see that her siblings would be properly dressed and cleaned up from head to toe. I also summoned Hunt to pick them up and get them to our wedding site. He told about the chain of events that followed, to just about anybody who would listen, many times over the years. Hunt would jokingly say, "I pulled up to Sue's house as agreed and was shocked back into reality. I blew my horn and out came five excited kids ranging in age from 10 to 15 years. I thought to myself, what am I doing? Am I crazy to do this again? Then as I drove past the Louisville airport, I was thinking that I should find a telephone booth, give them a quarter to call their mother, and get on the first flight to Tulsa. But that was just a tempting yet fleeting consideration."

Nonetheless, as I mentioned earlier, we simply joined in on my niece's wedding plans. Of course, we were welcomed in. We even received a couple of wedding gifts. After we had opened one gift and thanked the giver, I opened a second one. Surprise! We received not one but two 4-slice toasters. I whispered to Hunt, "We can return one of them." He replied, "Why? After all, there are seven of us now. We can use them both at the same time and we'll have seven slices of toast…one slice for each of us." So we kept both toasters and I secretly thanked him for his wisdom every time they were used.

After the ceremony, we returned to my house on Gregg Avenue that would now be our home. It was official…the children had a dad and I had a mate for life. And yes, they began addressing him as "Daddy" right away. All of them except Debby that is, who insisted to calling him *Mr. Hunt.* In regard to her manner of addressing him, he said, "I don't care what she calls me as long as she calls me in time to eat." We had many in-depth conversations before we committed to each other concerning what we wanted this marriage to be. We both agreed that God's Word would be our "go to source" whenever we needed answers. We would respect each other's opinions and be willing to compromise. We would try our best to mold the family into one unit. By this, we meant that the prefix "step" would not be used because we both saw it as a point of division. We also agreed to not override the decision one of us would make when the other party had previously said "No." We were committed to make this work, since we had both been burned several times.

Hunt and I were married for only two months when I discovered I was pregnant. I wanted to give him a child, but not this quickly. And what happened to that doctor's warning about the side effects of the treatment I had years ago for thyroids? Well, evidently becoming sterile was not in the cards for me. It wasn't that bad though. My biological clock was ticking and the time for me to bear children, I thought, was running out. When I told the kids I was expecting, they were ecstatic. Their reaction was mild compared to Hunt's. Never in his wildest dreams could he have imagined this happening to him. The news of my pregnancy served to bring us closer. I was so happy that I was able to give him a child! But our delight was short lived. I suffered a miscarriage four months later. My doctor gave me a clean bill of health and told me to wait six months, then try again.

The month of August had always been hot, but I believe the Lord sent a special heatwave. Our home on Gregg Avenue didn't have air conditioning. We only had electric fans to "cool" us (and I use that word loosely.) For months, I had been sticking to my guns about moving into his beautiful empty house on Jewell Avenue. I didn't have a good reason not to; it was just a feeling I had. One afternoon after working all day in an air conditioned school building and driving home in an air conditioned car, we opened the front door and heat, real heat, hit us in the face. Hunt looked at me and asked, "Do you want to take one more look at the house on Jewell Avenue?" To that I answered, "Yes. It couldn't hurt to look."

We loaded up the children and went to examine what might be our new home. When Hunt opened the front door, cold refreshing air leaped out at us and we were sold. I always believed that Hunt had gone there earlier in the day and lowered the thermostat on the AC to persuade me to cave in. However, he never owned up to it. So we packed up the house and moved into our new more spacious home. It had four bedrooms, living room, formal dining room, kitchen, a bath and a half, a full basement, large front porch and a small back porch. Plenty of good room for all. Hunt and I took the front bedroom on the first floor and used the other downstairs bedroom as a family room. The kids slept upstairs: the two girls on the front side and the three boys on the rear side with a half bath and large walk-in closet situated between their rooms. This would later become the focal point of many agreements as well as disagreements. All was well, but we had one point of contention. We didn't have our dog, Butch. When asked about it, Hunt implied that there was no room in the moving truck for him, but I knew he really didn't like for dogs to be confined to city living. He thought it was cruel to have them tied up and fenced in. In addition, unbeknownst to the children, he would say, "Two things I can't stand to be in my house--preachers and dogs, in that order." I knew he was joking, but now I had to look at five long, sad faces who were probably thinking that maybe their new dad wasn't so great after all.

Three days had passed when I heard joyful shouts coming from the front yard. Daddy was home and he had Butch with him in his truck! It turned out that Butch had been hit by a car and couldn't be located for a few days. Hunt had asked people in the old neighborhood to look out for Butch and to call him if he came back home. Faith in their dad was once again restored.

Picture us, a blended African American family moving into this beautiful home located in a previously all-white neighborhood. Our new home was located within walking distance to an 18-hole golf course and only a few blocks away from Shawnee Park in Louisville's West End. Segregation was still alive and well in the 1970s when we occupied our home on Jewell Avenue, so we were aware of the improbability of getting into this previously white locality. It became less difficult as a result of white flight—"the migration of large-scale, middle-class white populations from racially-mixed urban regions to more racially homogeneous suburban regions. Racial segregation of public schools had ended with the US Supreme Court's decision *Brown vs Board of Education* in 1954. However, in the 1970s attempts to achieve effective desegregation by means of forced busing in some areas led to more families moving out of former areas." *(Wikipedia)* Our family would experience both the negative and positive effects of forced busing.

For the next two years, money was tight in our family of seven. We took on a large paper route with *The Louisville Times/Courier Journal Newspaper* and delivered papers twice a day: *The Courier Journal on* weekday mornings and Sundays and delivering *The Times* every afternoon. We had to work as a team which meant everyone had a specific job to do--even Keith was not exempt. Shortly after we moved from Gregg to Jewell Avenue, he sustained life-threatening injuries while commuting back to his school. Keith was getting off a city bus when he was struck by automobile as he stepped in the crosswalk. Hunt and I were working at JAVS when we got the call; he rushed over to pick me up. Not knowing just how badly Keith was hurt made the 20-block drive seem to go on forever. Then came the wait for Keith to come out of surgery for the removal of his spleen. Keith's injuries were major—a broken pelvis along with multiple breaks in his right leg. Once he got out of the hospital he got up every morning and came along with his family to fold papers. All we could do was carry on as best as we could. We had a 1954 truck that Hunt drove while I drove the blue station wagon. The federally sponsored program at Jefferson Area Vocational School ceased to be funded. I found employment at Fort Knox in the Accounting and Finance Department. Since I worked at Fort Knox Army Base which was thirty miles away, their Aunt Maxie drove them on their route weekdays. Each Sunday we delivered over 500 papers, returned home, and got ready for church.

Even so, we still had to watch our outgo of money very carefully. Thank God, we had access to the Commissary at Fort Knox and we had an upright freezer. I can recall the standard shopping list I used every two weeks comprised the following items: 12 loaves of bread, 12 dozen eggs, 12 one-half gallons of milk, 12 pounds of bacon and/or sausage, along with other necessities.

Finances were about to improve; the $125/divorce settlement was about to end, but we still had to continue working hard to make ends meet. That meant having a large paper route while attending to the chores that needed to be done. The children were wonderful in helping, especially the three older ones. Debby was turning out to be a great cook. So much so that Hunt gave her a small stipend each week for making breakfast before going to school and for preparing dinner for the family each night. Dinner was special time in our home. It was always at six o'clock evening except on the Sundays we ate at Mama's house. Community leaders were made aware that it was important for our children to be home at that time for dinner. Social and school activities took a back seat when it came to family matters. When you hear someone refer back to *the "good ole days",* this is what they mean...a simpler time when people strived to keep families intact. The set dinner time definitely applied to every family member- no exceptions. The rule that I enforced before I met and married Hunt was that if you missed 6:00 p.m. dinnertime, you'd have to wait to eat until breakfast. Needless to say, I didn't have to make an example of an infraction but once, although nothing would stop common mishaps from occurring. Rodney writes:

BROKEN LAMP

One thing in our family that I could always count on is that my brothers and sisters stick together. I learned this truth

fairly early in my childhood. If I was in a tough situation, they proved they would come through for me. In short, I had broken one of Mama's favorite lamps. I was convinced in my young mind that this lamp was beyond repair. However, to my amazement, my siblings helped me repair the lamp and keep this mishap a secret for several years.

It all began in the summer of 1971. Mom and Dad had gone to work and left us at home with our daily chores. There were standing house rules to follow and Debbie, being the oldest, was always put in charge. We basically knew what to do and what not to do when Mom and Dad were away. Well, on this day our chores were done and we were all going about doing our own thing around the house. I'm not sure exactly what I was doing at the time, but I do know I was running through the house (most likely being chased by my brother Glenn). I found myself sprinting into the living room heading toward the front door when I bumped into Mom's favorite lamp. It went crashing to the floor! The lamp shattered into what I thought was a million pieces. I knew I was in big trouble and could only cry out "What to do, what to do, what to do!". Mom is going to be so angry and a whoopin' was coming my way tonight.

My sisters and brothers hurried into the living room to see what had happened. "Shocked" is the only way to explain their expression. However, after examining the situation they figured we can fix this. Realizing that Mom would be home in a few hours, we went to work. Somebody rushed to find the Elmer's Glue, while the rest of us begin picking up the pieces. The top and bottom of the lamp remained pretty much intact. It was the center multicolor glass body of the lamp that was the real challenge. Debbie and Del led the way gluing the pieces back together. Keith, Glenn and I searched the floor for every little piece we could find. I couldn't believe that this lamp was coming back together. "Oh no, we were almost out of glue!" What now? Well Debbie, aka: Susie homemaker, remembered a way to make homemade glue using products like flour and baking powder. Now we were back to work and before long the lamp was back together with the exception of one small piece no bigger than a quarter. We searched everywhere for that last piece, but it was nowhere to be found.

Now it was getting close to the time Mom gets home. We needed to make a decision. Do we tell Mom what happened to the lamp or do we keep it a secret between us and pray that she doesn't find out? A great deal was at stake. If we told Mom, everyone knew I would be in big trouble, and would probably not see the light of day for the rest of the summer. However, if we keep it a secret, and Mom found out, we would all be guilty of lying and conspiracy to hide the truth. To my amazement, my sisters and brothers decided to take a chance and not tell Mom what happened to the lamp. Suddenly, Glenn thought of something that just might work. He remembered that when the cap was left off of Crest toothpaste, it would get really hard…like cement. He leaped into action and carefully molded the toothpaste into the missing space; he got his school paint set and painted it perfectly. The lamp was put back in place.

About twenty years went by before Mom knew that her precious lamp had survived major surgery and was restored after being broken into thousands of pieced. The lamp was moved from Louisville to Owensboro before being sold in a yard sale. Mom could not believe that we had kept this secret for so long and the lamp stood the test of time. This story proves our family really can stick together.

Hunt had already taken another job that had a larger salary and plenty of fringe benefits. One day, he casually mentioned that he had an interview at Rohm and Haas Chemical Plant. When I asked him what he'd be doing, he answered, "Electrical work." Shocked, I said, "I didn't know you knew anything about electrical things. It was just one more thing I was to learn about him. But I should have known that he had received various kinds of training during his 20-year career in the Army.

That clock of mine wasn't ticking as fast as I thought it was, because after waiting six month we tried again with successful results. I was thirty-nine years old and pregnant. This time I vowed take better care of my precious package. During the previous pregnancy we all were working hard to stay afloat financially…especially with the paper route. I surely didn't want to experience the grief of losing a child prematurely again. The entire household took on an aura of excitement that I will never forget. The girls, Debby and Del, said, "If it's a girl, she's ours." While the boys said, "If it's a boy, he's ours." I laughed at them arguing over the sex of our unborn child, but was thrilled to see they cared so much about it. Hunt asked me if I wanted to continue working after the baby was born. I thought to myself, "What? Stop working? Never in my wildest dreams could I have imagined having the luxury of not working. I had resigned myself to the fact that I would always have to work to take care of my children. Now, here he stood asking me if I want to be a *stay-at-home mom.*" I pinched myself back into reality. He was waiting for an answer so I replied, "Yes, honey. I'd would love it." I tendered my resignation at Fort Knox when I reached my six month of pregnancy; I didn't want to take any undue chances with this child's development.

A healthy baby girl was born to our union on May 8, 1972 at Fort Knox Hospital. The girls won out. We named her Alyssa Joy but would call her "Joy." Of course, I was overjoyed for Hunt as I presented him with his first child. And no, I definitely didn't name her "the last" simply because I knew another child was not on our agenda. Hunt called her his *little bug-bug* which was no surprise since he was in the habit of giving a nick name to everybody. (He really got serious about nicknaming when the grandkids started coming.) Just like Debbie and Del had said they would, Baby Joy spent most of her time upstairs in their bedroom where she received the best of care with my "supervision".

Debbie graduated from High School two weeks after Joy was born. She was seventeen and that summer began working at the same shirt factory where I worked after my high school graduation. However, she decided to take a different path and entered the United States Air Force upon turning eighteen.

Rodney and Del were thrust into a life-threatening situation when the Louisville Board of Education instituted forced busing as a means to integrate public schools. In 1975 Rodney was to enter the ninth grade and Del the tenth grade at Pleasure Ridge Park High School. The City of Louisville was in an uproar with people showing their disapproval to the law picketing with signs and screaming ugly remarks at the students traveling by bus, sometimes five or ten miles, to attend class. Parents on both sides of the decision voiced their opinions openly which caused more division along racial lines. Of course, the thing that concerned black families was the personal safety of their children. My two teens had to be taken to a designated area to catch their bus that was equipped with four-inch, bullet-proof Plexiglas around all the windows for their protection. It was like they were prepared to go into a war zone and it proved to be necessary. Everyday our local newspaper reported injuries sustained by our children along with the violent acts aimed at them. This was surely a time to fervently pray for God's protection.

I wrote earlier that our family would experience both the negative and positive effects of forced busing. The negative part of busing was the danger they faced every day until people began to calm down. Nonetheless, I felt that the positive aspects of busing outweighed the negative ones in most cases. Before busing, one could readily see that the schools in the black neighborhood were inadequately staffed, the facilities outdated, and subject matter being taught was not up to par with schools located in predominately white neighborhoods. Delphia had always had a talent for and an interest in music. At Pleasure Ridge she had the opportunity to develop her gift. And Rodney would have never had an opportunity to take flying lessons at his former school. Courses like aviation were non-existent. They both graduated from Pleasure Ridge. I'd like to think that Del and Rodney were the front-runners to change that was definitely on its way. An article in *The Atlantic* entitled, "The City that Believed in Desegregation" states that "ever since a court forced them to integrate in the 1970s, the city of Louisville and surrounding Jefferson County had tried to maintain diverse schools. Though the region fought the integration at first, many residents and leaders came around to the idea and even defended it all the way up to the Supreme Court in 2006. Today the Louisville area is one of the few regions in the country that still busses student among urban and suburban neighborhoods. Presently, Jefferson County Public Schools are 49 percent white, 37 percent black, and 14 percent Latino and other ethnic and racial groups." (Alana Semuels)

Revival began at Central Baptist Church in the fall that year and members were thrust into an effort to reach the lost for Christ, and to bring slothful members of our fellowship back in, along with the unchurched. I had become accustomed to the fact that Hunt was not interested in attending, so the kids and I would go, leaving him home to care for the baby. After hearing the evangelist on the first night, I came home excited about the preacher's ability to deliver a spirit-filled, evangelistic message. He was an awesome speaker and I wanted so much for Hunt to hear him. I came home from the first night of revival fired up. So much so that I couldn't keep it to myself. I shared with him much of what I gotten out of the message and asked if he wanted to go the next night. He declined. The following night I did the same and he listened, but declined again. On the third night of revival as the children and I were getting dressed to go, he spoke up and asked, "What am I going to wear?" Those words happily flowed from his lips and we all started jumping around and shouting with joy. God did a work in his heart that night, in fact- in both of our hearts. We rededicated ourselves to Him that evening and never looked back. Hunt joined the fellowship of my home church and we were now all members of the same local body. All five of the older children had been baptized at an earlier time.

December was fast approaching and my favorite holiday, Christmas, was almost here. It was a special time of reflection, especially this year.

MY BEST CHRISTMAS

Growing up, my family always made a big deal out of Christmas even when times were very tough. The house would be filled with the smell of cakes and cookies baking.

I recall as a child how I looked forward to decorating the cookies. And we always had a real tree. The fragrance of pine would magically intermingle with the aroma coming from the kitchen. Luke's account of Jesus' birth was read every Christmas eve along with the poem "Twas the Night Before Christmas." The younger children then hurried off to bed and tried to fall asleep as fast as they could. They sure didn't want Santa to come and find them awake. The next morning, we woke to the smell of bacon cooking and knew that was our signal to come see what was under the tree. Gifts…there was always gifts for everyone. Quite a number of the gifts were homemade, but we were thankful for each gift we got. We were taught gifts were a representative of Jesus—God's gift to us. It was awesome!

Now, fast forward forty plus years to a very new phase in my life. I had met and married the man of my dreams. He was indeed a Godsend—strong, dependable and handsome to boot. He seemed to always have money in his pocket and lots of it. (That made him even more attractive.) I knew all the important things about him, but there were quite a few items about him I would learn later. He was quiet but very observant.

Evidently, he had noticed that our kitchen light needed attention because we were always changing the light bulb. So, he bought a new light fixture, and proceeded to test the electrical wires while I stood there with my mouth open, thinking, "Is he an electrician or do all men know how to do these things?" This was all new to me since we had always lived in the projects and when something needed fixing, we'd call the maintenance man.

Our first Christmas that year was wonderful and enjoyed by five children ranging from age 10 to 14 ½ years. They all had gifts under the tree; I had gotten a gift for Hunt; each of the children had given me a gift, but there was nothing for me from my new husband. I sought out a private time to mention it to him and to my surprise he answered, "But I gave you a new fluorescent light for the kitchen." Stunned, I thought to myself, "He's got a lot to learn." Next Christmas would be different.

Everything was going along just fine without any major problems when about two weeks before Christmas we experienced a leakage in the bathroom. So much so that the vanity cabinet and flooring had to be replaced. But the most urgent business was the replacement of the faulty pipes. Hunt went to the hardware store and secured what he needed to repair the leakage. He gathered up his plumbing tools and quietly went to work while I watched in amazement pondering, "I know he knows about electrician-type stuff, but is he a plumber, too?" I had so much to learn about the man I've been married to for less than two years. However, he did remember the previous Christmas oversight and told me in advance (after he had repaired the plumbing, purchased a new vanity and put down new floor covering) "Merry Christmas."

Christmastime on our third year was among one my best Christmases ever. A seven-month old baby girl had been added to our family and was crawling around pulling down every ornament she could reach. At this point, I didn't care what, if anything, I got for Christmas...I had it all. Gifts had been opened and shared. Everyone was about to scatter about to call their friends and such when Hunt picked up the baby, got our attention, and began to speak. He pulled out a beautiful card, gave it to me and began reading a letter that he had composed. Before long, we all knew the subject matter was "time." I wish I had the foresight to keep this letter in a physical safe place, but I didn't. However, I kept the words and phrases he wrote safely in my heart. It was beautifully written with phrases like there is a time for everything in every season; my time began when you came into my life; time stood still when I first saw you; I will love you for all time. He *stood up, came over to me, kissed me, and gave me the most beautiful watch I had ever received.*

Hmm. I hit the jackpot…an electrician, a plumber, and a writer.

By mid-1973, our family size was down to seven and that old blue station wagon was on its last leg. It was time to buy a new car or should I say station wagon. One thing for sure, it had to be spacious enough to hold the entire family comfortably. Our choice was an eight-passenger red Ford station wagon. Hunt said, "It's time to try it out on the road. Where do you want to go?" We decided to go to Oklahoma and boy, was that a trip! (No pun intended.)

OFF WE GO

"It was the best of times" wrote Charles Dickens in The Tale of Two Cities. For me that describes my sentiments at this period in my life with a little alteration. It was one of the best times, so far.

The summer of 1973 found the Hunt/Davis crew doing well. Everybody was healthy, wise and a bit wealthier. Debby had completed her basic training in the Air Force and had moved on for further training. Besides, we were contemplating enjoying a long ride to Oklahoma in our spanking-new car, an eight passenger Ford station wagon. On our first trip to Hunt's home state, we stayed with his brother, Lewis and wife Margaret along with their four children. We arranged to bunk with them again, which was ideal since we were all about the same age. In fact, I was only a few months older than Lewis.

The road trip from Louisville to our Oklahoma destination would take a full two days. Our itinerary was to leave home on Thursday morning, drive to Paducah, Kentucky and spend the night with two of our friends, start out early Friday morning and travel for approximately eight hours on I-44 West to Tulsa. Actually, Hunt had allowed two more additional hours to accommodate frequents stops we'd take. We would stay in Tulsa for a period of two weeks. I was in charge of supervising the packing. With six of us to pack for and one-year-old Joy still in diapers, I knew I had to pack as lightly as possible. As we began bringing our suitcases out to the car, reality set in. Where would we ride? There wasn't enough room in the car for all the bags and us.

Hunt was still inside the house checking security and such, when we made a unanimous decision. Our station wagon was equipped with luggage racks on top, so we could put the bags up there. That would make room for Joy's milk and diapers to be kept inside. Dad and I would sit up front, of course; Keith and Del would sit on the middle seat so Del could see after baby Joy; Glenn and Rodney could sit on the back row. Perfect! Until somebody asked, "Where's Grandma gonna sit?" "Oh no," I cried, "I forgot to make room for Mama." I did tell you Mama was going, too, didn't I? She was looking forward to meeting Hunt's mother. Her theory was that if you met one's mother, you could tell a lot about a man's character. (This tradition began with Mama and continues to be practiced in our family to this day).

The seating order had to be changed to accommodate her, so Keith, Glenn, and Mama would ride on the second seat while Del and Rodney, the two smallest, shared the back row to attend to Joy. To our dismay, we definitely hadn't thought it through fully, because when Hunt came out of the house and saw what we'd done, he was dumbfounded. He said, "Just

103

how do you think those bags will fare up there on top with wind and possible rain hitting them?" We stood there frozen and speechless until Glenn suggested covering them with plastic drop cloths. Hunt replied, "I guess that will have to do until we can buy something more sustainable like tarpaulin and some stronger rope."

So off we go to Grandma's house to pick her up. Out comes my seventy-six year- old mother with her luggage. I looked at Hunt's face and thought he was surely going to break into tears when he saw the amount of bags she had-- two pieces of luggage and two large hat boxes. Oh my! Mama was a fashionable dresser and she always wore a hat to church. We'd be gone for two weeks so that meant two church services with a different hat for each. Mama's hats had to ride in the rear with the baby's diapers. So off we went again, looking like the Beverly Hillbillies.

We had only traveled some twenty miles when the loud thumping began. Wind had gotten under the bags and they were flopping up and down like crazy. Thump, thump, thump, so much so that Hunt had to pull over on I-64 to secure them. The plastic cloth covering on the bags was torn into shreds and had to be removed. It was quiet for now, but after another fifty miles the noise started once more. This time it was the weak rope that had loosened. Hunt and the older boys tightened the rope and we set out again hoping that nothing else would prevent us from reaching our first stop.

My friends, Thomas and Essie greeted us with welcome arms and a good meal. A four-hour trip to Paducah was lengthened to a six-hour one, but we were thankful to have arrived there safely and with luggage still on top. Through all of this, not a word of complaint emanated from my mother. After dinner, Thomas and Hunt went to Walmart to buy the tarp and rope then returned to anchor the bags down properly. We left early the next morning as planned crossing a small portion of Illinois and onto through Missouri on highway 44 West. All without a peep from the bags on top. The scenery on I-44 was awesome especially going through the Mark Twain National Forest.

As we arrived in Oklahoma, we could visualize Native Americans coming over the mountains onto the flat landscape. What an entertaining sight it was to see the buffalo roaming the fields for our first time- something we'd only seen in the movies. The countryside seemed to go on for miles after miles until we finally saw the skyline of Tulsa. After greeting each other and settling in, Margaret noticed that we, mostly Del, had been carrying Joy around and asked her why. I responded, "She's not walking yet." She replied, "What? She walked into the house by herself and down the hallway." All of them insisted that it was true. Joy had taken her first steps and we had all missed it. However, after her first stroll, she never walked alone again until she was almost one and a half. Joy had us all fooled; she could walk, but why should she if we were willing to carry her? Smart girl.

During the next two weeks, we crammed everything we could into our stay. We played, cooked, toured, rode horses, and fished. Soon it was time to make the long trip home and pack up the car again. Lewis suggested that we'd ship our luggage back to Louisville on the Greyhound Bus Lines. What God-given advice that was! And one we hopped on without giving it another thought. So we bought packing boxes and shipped all our clothing in them; the boxes would arrive in Louisville before we got home. I should say we packed 'almost' everything. Joy's necessities and, of course, Mama's hats had to travel in the car with us.

So, off we went again…this time headed for home. We could hardly believe how comfortable the ride home was with plenty of good room for everybody to stretch out. Lewis and Margaret had packed up some goodies for us to eat along the way. Being the wonderful griller he claimed to be, we knew there would be some food he had cooked on the grill. On our way back, Hunt announced that we would stop at a state park that ran along Interstate 44. Twin Bridges State Park in Missouri was chosen. It was well-equipped with tables, benches and grills to barbecue on. I would recommend this park as a beautiful place with much to see. We saw two deer up close and personal along with some exotic animals and plants. Our adventurous journey was over and it was time to return home.

Upon arriving back home again, I knew the time had come to reveal my closely held secret. I was five months pregnant! And this time I was definitely not a happy camper. I was too old to have another baby. My goodness, I had a daughter serving in the United States Air Force. What would she think? What would everyone think? I delayed telling Debby that I was having another baby, but when I did, she asked, "Mother, are you happy?" I replied, "Yes, I'm very happy." To which she said' I don't care how many babies you have as long as you're happy." Her words were music to my ears and lessened my anxiety a bit. Nonetheless, the idea of another pregnancy threw me into a slight depression. This child would be my seventh.

Adding to my depression was the memory of a statement I confronted my mother with when I was a teenager. I recall asking Mama, "Why would you or anybody ever have seven children?" I was immediately convicted by those words. I was <u>her</u> seventh child. What was I doing, questioning my own existence? I quickly apologized-thanking her for giving me life. Now, I began to think that the flood gates had reopened and had a real moment of déjà vu. Yes, I've done this before… having five children in just over five years. But I was young then; was a forty-one-year-old now.

During the following months, I tried to no avail to shield my increasing weight from view with large over-sized clothing. I told everyone my weight gain could be attributed to a medical condition—I had a kidney problem, of sorts. Hunt was no help at all. He jokingly compared us to Sarah and Abraham, but I knew he was excited at the prospect of having another child. On October 16 of that year, I delivered my *kidney problem* --a 10 lb. 3 oz. baby boy. The nurses at the hospital had already named him Rosey Grier after a well-known 284 lb. football star, Roosevelt Grier.

Hunt and I had many long discussion about what to name the baby if it were a boy. I was not fond of his first name, Willard, and didn't know he had a middle name, since NMI (no middle initial) was on his military records. Now the truth came out. He did have a middle name; it was Neil and that settled it for me. We'd name him Willard Neil Hunt, Jr. and would call him Neil. Finally conceding, he explained why he didn't like his middle name and therefore refused to use it. Negative memories went all the way back to when he was young and had a very strict school principal named Miss Neal. Hunt was left handed and Miss Neal would use every method available to make him right-handed. Striking him on his hands was her favorite thing to do. She felt it was necessary that he reform because all the classroom desks were for right-handed students. The punishment ceased when Hunt's mother got word of what was happening to him. Using his given middle name was not an option for him even though it was spelled differently. The boys had gotten their wish this time and baby Neil was soon moved upstairs with them.

Let me explain what moving my babies upstairs with the teenage/preteens meant. (Debby was still in the mix until she left for the military.) They agreed to change their diapers, to feed them, and to comfort them when they cried, while still maintaining good grades in class. The agreement would become null and void if their grades began to decline. It goes without saying that I thought the agreement was wonderful. In fact, having built-in babysitters proved to be even more awesome!

Looking at my husband's face and seeing the happiness and peace exuberating from him was something to behold. He finally had the children he'd prayed for and I was the agent God used to provide them for him. Hunt continually surprised me with his hidden skills and abilities. Many of them were used to expand God's work at church and in the community. Our Pastor noticed how he fervently served others and appointed him as a deacon.

Then on one Sunday afternoon after church service, he cornered me in our bedroom and said that we needed to talk. We sat on the edge of the bed and he told me of his desire to go back to school. I agreed that would be great, especially since he hadn't used his GI bill yet. Then I asked, "Are you thinking of getting a degree as an electrician?" Hunt answered, "No. I'm considering a degree in theology." I said, "The...who?" Hunt slowly answered, "T h e o l o g y." And went on to explain how he arrived at this decision, saying: "Ever since my conversion when I was thirty years old, I have been having these recurring dreams or visions of standing in front of a group of people speaking to them. Each time I spoke, several things remained the same. I loved doing it; I understood and was excited about the subject matter; and I was trying very hard to get the listeners to see my point and react. This scenario repeated itself over and over again. When

I became a sergeant in the Army and was given more duties that involved public speaking, I said to myself *that's it,* but the dreams didn't stop. Then when I started teaching at the vocational school, I felt sure that the visions would come to an end, but they didn't stop, they only became more vivid. Baby, I have surrendered my life to the Lord to use and He has called me into the preaching ministry. I accepted His call to the ministry and the dreams have ceased." He paused to get my reaction. I grabbed him and held him close and with tears of joy welling up in my eyes, I expressed my agreement with his decision while going on to tell him that I had always felt God wanted me to be a pastor's wife and now it appears to be coming into fruition.

The next Sunday, he stood before the congregation of Central Baptist Church and acknowledged his call to preach the gospel. A few weeks later, Hunt preached his trial sermon. After the members had finished voting to license him, I'll never forget my mother shouting out, "Loose him and let him go." It was certainly a joyful, unforgettable moment as he knew he definitely had Mama's approval. The next step for him was to enroll in Simmons Bible University and he wasted no time in doing so.

All was fine at Central Baptist Church until Hunt enrolled in college. Central's pastor had not attained a degree in religious studies; he had only take a few classes, just enough to get him by. All this was public knowledge, but envy didn't rise to the front until a young, up-and-coming minister was now in the ranks. Simply saying, the green-eyed monster showed its face. Meanwhile, Hunt was excited about sharing what he learned at school, so whenever he had an opportunity to teach Sunday School or Wednesday night Bible studies, he did. Before long, verbal confrontations made it impossible for us to remain at our home church. It was unnatural for us to come home from church with headaches, but we did and knew it was time for us to go.

Our intentions were to begin visiting several other local churches in the community, but after worshipping one Sunday in a church just two blocks away from Central, our search was over, West End Baptist Church. Hunt and I were convinced this was where God wanted us to be. However, we wanted our children to be in agreement with us and they were. We returned to West End the next week and when we pulled into the parking lot, Joy began to cry, "I don't want to go to this Baptist church!" She was just over two years old, but observant enough to realize the difference in atmosphere that existed between the two churches. West End's building was much smaller with lower ceilings which made the enthusiastic congregational singing ring out louder. Truthfully speaking, you couldn't hear people singing at Central Baptist if you were standing next to them. It hadn't always been that way, but as the church decreased in membership, so did its zeal. We all tried to comfort Joy holding her closely to us. She soon calmed down after she saw how much we were enjoying the fellowship. When the invitation was extended, all eight of us went forward to join. It would be the best decision we would make and the highlight of our Christian life.

Lincoln Bingham was the pastor of West End; his wife's name was Lillian. And boy, they were a terrific couple who truly loved the Lord and His people. Lincoln was well-known in Kentucky and its surrounding states. He had a vision for church growth and was before its time. Lincoln also served as Director of Missions with the Southern Baptist Convention which provided our church to be duly aligned with both the Southern and Progressive National Baptist Conventions. Hunt became one of the associate ministers serving along with several others. Because of Rev. Bingham's association with the Baptist Theological Seminary in Louisville, he was able to draw young students from the seminary to West End, taking them under his supervision and providing some much needed on-the-job experience. Hunt was one of about eight other ministers receiving this training.

I was soon hired as secretary of West End and worked there weekdays until two o'clock which got me home before school let out. Joy and Neil attended a Christian nursery school at Baptist Fellowship Center. They loved it. One day they brought home a page they had colored containing a blessing. Of course, Joy, being older, colored hers perfectly while Neil's wasn't as professionally done. They both got praised for doing a great job. The blessing read: *Dear Lord, We are thankful for all your loving care...for love, for home, for family, and food for us to share. Amen.* It fit our family perfectly in that for the past generations our family had exhibited its gift of hospitality to all who came within our reach. Moreover, my mother had been faithful in perpetuating hospitality through each family member. So we adopted this prayer and made it our family prayer that we continue to use today. Anyone joining our family by birth, marriage, or "adoption" must learn this prayer to be an official member.

Hunt was ordained by West End Baptist Church on October 3, 1976 and received a Bachelor of Theology degree from Simmons University on May 24, 1982. Note: he graduated top of his class. After his ordination, he became known as *Will the Baptist* due to his regularity in being chosen to perform the baptism rite so effortlessly. Here is a story I wrote that will shed some light onto what was occurring at this point in our family life.

A FULL HOUSE

The little white frame church "with all those little children" was growing by leaps and bounds. Pastor Lincoln had a growth vision for West End Baptist Church that was surely inspired. Many people came to join wanting to learn and to get closer to the Lord; therefore, a plan was put in place to minister to each member. All this was made possible by an upsurge in students from the Southern Baptist Theological Seminary in Louisville. It appeared that word reached every incoming student of the seminary about the friendliness of West End and the welcoming, unselfish pastor who provided everyone opportunity to grow. The design called for an associate minister and a deacon to team up together as family leaders; they were assigned alphabetically. This arrangement provided time for the Pastor to concentrate on weightier matters. My husband was one that ministered to families whose last name began with letters G to I.

I can only verify that the arrangement worked excellently for the Hunt family as I tell you about what occurred in our home every Sunday afternoon. We always had "guests" eating with us and then staying in place until the six o'clock evening worship began. Most were ministers and missionaries along with our choir pianist, Pauline. Guests were only called guests for the first fifteen minutes of the first visit, after that time you were no longer viewed as one. After eating and maybe watching a little TV, they usually found a comfortable place to nap. Each occasion to gather was packed with many memorable moments. Here are a few incidents that are my favorites:

Ricaldo Phillips was a young student who came from Antigua to prepare for the ministry. I was intrigued by the tone of his voice, because I never expected to hear such a strong English accent coming from him. I had judged his origin of birth by the color of his skin. Ricaldo would naturally be considered to be an African American on first sight, but when he opened his mouth to speak all doubts disappeared. He stood less than six feet in height and weighed approximately 160 lbs. I learned an important cultural fact on the first Sunday he was at our home.

Places were set for eight people at our main dining room table, so adjustments had to be made according to who showed up. The adults would usually sit in the dining area while youngsters sat at the kitchen table. A fold-up table was provided to hold the food and everyone could serve their own plate, banquet style.

It wasn't until we all sat down at the table that I noticed how much Ricaldo had put on his dinner plate. Of course, I didn't mind the amount; even so, I wondered if he'd be able to consume all of it. I kept a close eye on him as he tried to devour everything he had on his plate. He was definitely struggling. That's when I spoke up and told him he didn't have to eat all the food he put on his plate. He replied, "Of a truth, of a truth." More time passed and if he could have, he would've turned green. When I spoke up more strongly, he put down his fork and apologized profusely. Then, he explained his dilemma saying, "In my culture, we are taught that it would be an insult to the hostess not to eat everything one puts on his plate and that you should take plenty. If you put it on, you must eat it. However, back home we have different sized plates to choose from ranging in dimension from saucers to platters. You had only one size. The Bible says that in all your getting, get an understanding. The next week, he put only what he could handle on his plate and all was well.

My two youngest children, Joy and Neil, sat at the kitchen table with three of their older siblings, Glenn, Del, and Rodney. They were really great babysitters and usually very attentive. Even so, some things just slip past the best of us. My husband, Hunt was seated at the head of the dinner table; I was on his right; and a visitor to our church who was on his left. When I looked up from my plate, I noticed a strange, uncomfortable look on the woman's face. I thought she had gotten something in her mouth that was distasteful, so I kept looking for further clues. That's when I noticed that the weird looks were aimed at my husband. Now I was truly confused. Just then we heard a commotion under the table. When I raised the tablecloth to look, there was Neil, my two-year-old son, quietly sitting there, stroking the woman's pantyhose. I grabbed him and asked him what he was doing under the table (as if I didn't know) and he said in his toddler's voice, "I like the way they feel." Needless to say, we all had a good chuckle as our guest breathed a sigh of relief.

During this period, two of my older children were often absent- Debby, who was serving in the Air Force, and Keith who was in college. Debby's picture in her uniform was displayed proudly on the mantelpiece for all to see. I believe that was the first thing that Carl, one of the ministers, saw of interest. Therefore, he began to inquire about her. I thought Carl was really handsome with his big smile and his pearly white teeth. I told Debby that he was asking about her and that she should talk to him. She said, "Didn't you say that he was a preacher? Well, first of all, I'm not interested in dating a preacher and then what's so special about his teeth…so white and strong? Is he a man or a horse? Not interested!" Nonetheless, Carl began to avail himself to talk every Sunday when Debby called. And she called regularly each Sunday. After the talks started, I just sat back and watched what the Lord was going to do or not do.

Debby came home on leave after a few months and they got acquainted. They became friends and dated some but it was not the Lord's will that they would be more than friends. They both found their life-long partners and both have been happily married for almost forty years.

Although there were many chances to grow and learn new skills, Glenn tells of one such opportunity that clearly stands out from his childhood memories. He wrote:

A MUCH NEEDED LESSON

I was about thirteen when Daddy came into the picture. It was an exciting time for me because some of the weight of protecting my siblings would be lessened. It wasn't long before I realized that my new dad knew a lot about everything, especially tools. I had a little knowledge of tools with an interest in learning more about them. What I knew about them I learned from my uncles. However, when Daddy came along he had all kinds of tools, tools I had never seen before and I was very interested in them.

One tool in particular peeked my interest; it was the torque wrench. It had a long pointed thing on one side, with a long list of numbers on it, and a wiggly handle. I tried to take it apart to see how it worked. In the process I bent the pointed thing so that it was set on 45 instead of zero. Later when Daddy went to his tool box, he immediately knew I had been messing with his tools. He came and asked me if I'd been playing with them. I hesitantly told him, "Yes.". He was not *angry about what I had done realizing I was just curious. That's when I got my first lesson from him. He spoke gently yet firmly, "If you're going to mess with tools, you ought to know how to use them.*

Now the tool you bent is called a torque wrench. It is used where the tightness of screws and bolts is crucial. It allows the operator to measure the strength applied to the fastener thus permitting proper tension to parts. So do you see why it is important that it's not bent?"

From that day on he took me under his wing and taught me all about tools- what tools are used for and how to save time using them. Because of his patient guidance, I became skilled in using all sorts of tools for electrical, auto mechanics, and carpentry. At the time, I didn't know how this knowledge would affect me in the future. Now when my grandkids ask me a question I patiently teach them remembering how Daddy patiently taught me.

So much of my life had changed. First of all, I had personally grown closer to God. The trials and seeming setbacks I had experienced ensured maturity was bound to occur. I know with all certainly that my trials only served to make me stronger. I guess that was one of the reasons that led us to walk in unity…we had both suffered the heartaches of rejection. Thank God we found each other.

Almost identical to the manner to which the first five of my children came into the world, they entered the adult world in the same order—within six years. Although, they always felt loved, we had devised a course of action to make sure they understood that their stay at home was temporary. We'd say, "After you reach age eighteen, you have three choices, go to college, join the military, or get a job." To reiterate our order, we'd have a *break your plate party,* during which we would have an awesome dinner with all the trimmings. Then afterwards, we'd take an old plate and break it symbolizing they've had a decision for future endeavors. It may have seemed cruel thing to do at times, but they all got the point.

Debbie joined the Air Force in 1972;

Keith entered Eastern Kentucky University in 1974;

Glenn joined the Army in 1976;

Del enrolled at Eastern Kentucky University in 1977;

Rodney enter Kentucky State University in 1978.

Every year following 1972, there was someone going away from home. It was an exciting time for us. Included in the mix was Hunt, since he began his studies of theology in 1974. Meanwhile, Joy and Neil were growing by leaps and bounds, but that didn't shield them from heartbreak of witnessing their brothers and sisters leave home so close together. The last one to leave for college was Rodney. Neil was four years old at the time. Up to now Neil was alright with the others departing. But now the drama would begin. Rodney had been packed up with Neil looking on; we had driven him fifty miles to KSU, taken his stuff up four flights of steps, but when we were about to say "Goodbye", Neil said, "Come on, Rodney; let's go home." We were all stunned and had to tell Neil that Rodney wasn't coming home with us. It seemed that he never understood that we would be leaving Rodney there. Neil cried so hard. Only his big brother's promise that he would come home regularly comforted him.

No one had left the home permanently and our rules we agreed upon years ago where still intact. Hunt was an advocate of higher education and was aware that none of the children could be successful without emotional and financial help from us. So while they matriculated, we sent them both money and care packages. And our efforts were not wasted.

- Debbie stayed in the air force for six years before enrolling in University of Louisville, 1978. During her tour, she had the grand opportunity to perform with U. S. Air Forces' top talents: Tops in Blue. Debby's educational attainment includes a degree in Occupational Therapy from Spalding University in 1995 and a master's degree two years later.

- Keith finished Eastern Kentucky University in 1980 and was commissioned as an officer in the U.S. Army. After entering the military in 1978 and spending four years active duty, Keith completed twenty years in the army reserve retiring with rank of Lieutenant Colonel.

- Glenn enlisted in the Army immediately after graduating in 1976 from Aarons Technical Trade School, and served seventeen years. He received an Associate's degree from Wallace College in Applied Science in 1996.

- Delphia completed two years at Eastern Kentucky University and in 1980 enlisted in the Air Force. She retired in 2000 after serving 20 years.

- Rodney completed his studies at Kentucky State University in 1982 graduating with an Accounting Degree and immediately began employment at Fort Campbell Army base where he continues to work today.

Meanwhile our involvement in the mission of West End Baptist was becoming more significant. Pastor Bingham found several opportunities for Hunt to get more experience serving local churches. Most involved serving in interim pastor positions while a membership looked for a permanent pastor. He was well-respected around the Louisville area and appreciated for his diligence in rightly dividing the Word of God. There were some who didn't appreciate his candidness, but that fact didn't deter him one bit. He just kept on being himself and aiming to please God.

Because of Pastor Bingham's position with the Southern Baptist Convention, he was privy to concerns and requests for assistance from associations in and around

Kentucky. Such a request had come to his attention. A small group of African American Christians had been gathering in a daycare center in Daviess County each Sunday to worship. They had called the SBC stating interest in using their study materials for missions and Sunday School. Lincoln was asked to find someone who was willing to guide them through the process and he approached Hunt with the opportunity and he agreed. The next week, we traveled one hundred miles to Owensboro, Kentucky to meet them for the first time.

We felt welcomed immediately as we entered the small but adequately-sized room with twelve smiling faces who comprised mostly family members. The daycare facility was owned and operated by Argatha Jackson. An old piano was available, so I could provide accompaniment for the group. Upstairs over the day care center was a suitable place for the four of us to sleep with a small kitchen. West End's members gave us a great send off as we were leaving for Hunt to serve as interim pastor, and the church was filled to capacity with well-wishers and family. When the time came for remarks, I remember my brother, Buckle, standing on his feet and with tears running down his face proclaiming these words regarding me, "Never in my wildest dreams would I have thought she'd turn out this good." My family joined in saying, "So true" "and Amen!" What could I say? I knew I was a little tyrant growing up.

On the following Saturday, we loaded up the kids and drove to Owensboro. I knew what this all meant to our family especially to Hunt. This would be his first real opportunity to pastor. Joy was almost eleven years old and Neil was nine years and a bit. I was thankful that there were at least two children their age in the group. After only a few weeks of meeting in the center, a church building became available for purchase. THE WESTERN RECORDER wrote a page-long article, February 16, 1983, on our new venture. I'd like to share some excerpts from it with you.

OWENSBORO EFFORT REACHES BEYOND COLOR LINES
BOLD MISSIONS IN BLACK AND WHITE

Two years ago, three women, Argatha Jackson, Hazel West, and Mildred Tinsley had an idea that turned into reality. They had been traveling twelve miles back and forth to their home church for several years when they realized their efforts were futile. The country church of their youth had decreased in membership over the years mainly because when the church's young people reached adulthood they fell into inactivity. Some moved to larger cities after completing their education. They met for the first time at the day care center on August 19, 1982. Soon it became clear the "family church" situation there would be impossible to get off the ground without some help.

They went to the Kentucky Baptist Convention asking for
assistance in establishing a Southern Baptist Church.
Everything began falling into place.

- *Willard Hunt, an associate minister of West End Baptist*
  Church in Louisville had been commuting for several
  weeks serving as Interim Pastor when they called him
  as their acting pastor.
- *Meanwhile there stood a vacant church building in*
  Owensboro, but even more importantly, it stood in an
  area where it seemed a new work would appeal to a
  number of lost and unchurched people. The facility
  would be called Cedar Street Baptist Chapel.

- *The owner wanted $40,000 with a $10,000 down*
  payment. Daviess-McLean Association appropriated an
  interest free loan of $5,000 and appointed Temple
  Baptist Church sponsor of the mission chapel. Temple's
  congregation gave $3,000 to the cause and Cedar
  Street raised the remaining $2,000.

Even though the chapel was not without its critics, it
became into being, and in doing so made history. Cedar
Street Baptist Chapel was the first black congregation in
Kentucky seeking to organize in cooperation with the state
convention and the local Southern Baptist Association.

Over time, the weekly commute back and forth to
Owensboro got to be laborious. God heard our cry. A large
apartment building right next to the Church was put up for
sale. It was such good timing we surely felt God leading us to
purchase it, so we met with the realtor, examined the property
and later, after counting up the cost, decided to buy. The
apartment building had a living room, four bedrooms, one and
a half baths, a very large kitchen/dining room area with new
appliances. This was the selling point for me. I especially
loved the 6-foot wide fireplace that divided the kitchen and

dining rooms. And this was just the main floor. On the second floor were three separate apartments—two were one-bedroom apartments and one had two bedrooms; all had full-sized kitchens with one bath. To top it off, all of the apartments upstairs were fully furnished. It couldn't get any better than this, we thought. We sold our home on Jewell Avenue and made the purchase. It was hard saying goodbye to the place that had provided so many beautiful, long-lasting memories, but we felt God's leadership guiding us forward.

In the 80's, Owensboro felt like a small rural town compared to Louisville. Since then it has grown tremendously making it the fourth largest city in Kentucky. We weren't aware of or did not experience any noticeable racial exclusion. We were treated warmly by most people. The exception was the pastors of the black congregations who seemed cool at first. Some of them warmed up to *the new pastor and family in town.* It wasn't long before we knew that it would be in ours or Cedar Street's best interest to keep our distance from local ministers. We are aware we couldn't get too friendly.

Corruption spewing from pulpits in the black community there was common knowledge, but was simply disregarded by the membership. There were only a couple of churches in the entire city that were not in that category. For example, one pastor had been arrested for stealing, was incarcerated but was let out of jail every Sunday to preach only to be returned to lock-up until the next Sunday. Another pastor had the reputation of sexual involvement with several young women under his leadership and had fathered children by some. All this happening with the knowledge and apparent "blessings" of his members. Yet another pastor was a known shoplifter of men's suits. All one had to do was to tell him the color and sized desired and he'd get for you. We were positive that God sent us to Owensboro to use us to show our lights to those living in darkness.

As we settled into our new home and new hometown, we first had to get our two youngsters situated in school. Joy was almost eleven finish the fifth grade while nine year old Neil was to finish fourth grade. Neither of them were thrilled about leaving their friends and school mates behind in Louisville and moving into a new town. However, Neil appeared to be more comfortable with the change than did Joy. Probably concerning her most was the thought of being placed in a regular classes resulting from the move, as some school systems had practiced. In Louisville, she had just been approved for placement in the gifted and talented program. She sure didn't want that to change.

Neil was smart and a good student, but wasn't that interested in school at this point of his development. He just missed his buddies and immediately found replacements. He and Paul, a new found neighbor, became especially close. Meanwhile Joy cried everyday concerning her dislike for Owensboro in general and her new school in particular. I felt it was time to pay a visit to the teacher in an effort to create a plan to get her more involved and excited about attending school again. The problem—the fifth grade class was learning what she had already learned in her class in Louisville…she was bored with nothing to do. The solution--the teacher devised individual lesson plans for her that included helping other students during class time and computer generated studies on a higher level for her. Joy wrote the following story about how our move to Owensboro affected her.

MISSING FRIENDS

I was in the fifth grade and was nearly 11 years old when my family moved from Louisville to Owensboro, KY. My father had been called to pastor a chapel in a new town and we all looked forward to this move with great anticipation. Once we arrived in Owensboro, my family and I went about the tasks of moving in, getting acquainted with our new schools and new neighbors. I made a few friends in the waning months of my fifth grade year. I was looking forward to starting the "Advanced Program" in the sixth grade and what new adventures middle school would bring.

A couple of weeks into the sixth grade, however, I realized that the exciting adventures I had expected would await me never materialized. Not only was I the only black girl in my grade in the Advanced Program, but I was still the "new girl" **and** *I was an outsider. I had trouble working my combination lock, so I carried all my books to every class. I stressed about making good grades. I sat alone at lunch. I had <u>no</u> friends. I was miserable, but I didn't want to trouble my parents about it. They'd been so excited about the move and the opportunity for Daddy to pastor a church. I decided to bottle up the stress I'd been feeling.*

A few weeks later while sitting in English class I started experiencing chest pains. It really scared me. I started to breathe more rapidly which only made the chest pains worse. My teacher took me to the nurse's office and the nurse immediately called my parents. My mother took me to the doctor that afternoon and he did an EKG and a complete medical work-up. Nothing was physically wrong with me. He asked me if there was anything bothering me and I revealed that I was really stressed about getting good grades. Mama set up appointments with my teachers so we could discuss my progress. Teacher after teacher told me that I either had A's or A+'s. I could tell that Mama was confused. When we got home from school, she asked me point blank, "Joy, what else is going on?" The floodgates opened. I sobbed. I told her about the locker, about not fitting in, about sitting alone at lunch and how I didn't have a single friend. Then, Mama told me something surprising. She said, "Joy, do you know that I don't have any friends here either?" I was shocked. I thought to myself, "How could Mama not have any friends? She makes friends everywhere she goes! Everybody loves Mama!"

"It's true," she said. I felt bad that I'd been so consumed by my own troubles that I didn't see her pain. We hugged each other and I cried some more. Then Mama said the most amazing thing to me: "Since you don't have a best friend and I don't have a best friend, why don't we vow to be each other's best friend?" "I'd like that, Mama." I said. She's been my best friend ever since.

By the end of my sixth grade year, I had made a few friends, but still had no close friends. I was getting used to Owensboro, but still certainly felt like an outsider. Most of the black girls in my grade looked at me with suspicion. I was accused of being an Oreo and of "trying to act white." I often fantasized about how great it would be to move back to Louisville where we had lots of family and friends. I was complaining about Owensboro to my parents one day when Mama made a joke about me staying in Owensboro. I said, "Nuh-unh! When I turn 18, I'm going to sell the house and move back to Louisville!" Mama asked, "Where will Daddy and I be? Dead!?" I thought to myself, "Oops. I hadn't thought about that part."

Glenn was serving overseas, so his wife, Geraldine (Gerrie), son, Markeese, and their infant daughter, Nikeiva, came to live with us in his absence. They occupied one of the second floor apartments. Looking back, I don't know how we could have made it without their love and support.

In the meantime, the ministry at the chapel was slowly growing with an attendance around thirty-five attending regularly. Hunt, of course, was handling all the spiritual needs of the congregation plus attending association meetings. The Bible teaches that the angels in heaven rejoice when one comes to Christ. Gerrie had earlier made a personal decision to follow Christ and now wanted to be baptized. She waited for Glenn to come home on leave so it could be done at West End. It turned out to be a two-fold celebration as Glenn joined her in rededication and in rebaptism. My duties at the Chapel mostly revolved around the music program and preparing weekly bulletins. It wasn't long before we formed a choir with somebody providing robes for each member. This was a biggie. One could see the look of accomplishment pasted on the members' faces. Having a formal choir led to inclusion into more fellowship opportunities with other churches, black and white.

Hunt and I began to notice a few areas of concern that were beginning to surface. We noticed some prevalent members wanted to return to some traditions they had said they wanted to leave behind. They were minute at first but if not addressed would become bigger, such as collecting weekly dues from choir members. When Hunt explained that there was no need for a separate treasury and that all money should go into the general fund, some did not like that at all. Hunt had taught many classes on tithes and offering which was the only biblical way to financially support the church. Eventually a meeting had to be called to address the issue. The deacons and trustees were all on one accord with the pastor. The budget and the plan on how they could successfully meet it was spelled out in detail. To sum it up,

Hunt stated, "If each member would support the budget by giving one-tenth of their increase, there would be more than enough money available to meet all the needs of our congregation without getting assistance from Temple, our sponsoring church. If there is someone who cannot at this time give a tithe and gives an offering regularly until he or she is able to do so, that too is satisfactory. However, we must be willing to give as the Lord has prospered us."

Then the unthinkable happened. An angry member spoke up loudly and clearly saying, "I don't care what the Bible says about tithing, I'm not going to do it!" The majority voted to not tithe. We looked at each other and without another word, adjourned the meeting.

Hunt and I discussed privately our next move. We felt we had just looked the devil in the face. Even now, I can still hear those words ringing in my ears. How could people who once seemed to be on fire for the Lord and in only two years turn around so quickly? Thank goodness it wasn't all of them...just the loudest. First thing the next morning, Hunt called his mentor and spiritual advisor, Rev. Bingham and after explaining what had blatantly happened the night before, he decided to offer his resignation effectively immediately. However he couldn't do so without notifying Temple Baptist Church pastor so he could alert the association. The following Sunday, he resigned as interim pastor. For all practical purposes, this ended our relationship with members of Cedar Street Chapel, although we still occupied the house next door. The take away from our experience there was a positive learning and growing one.

So we had to regroup. Due to an economic downturn occurring in the mid-eighties, our finances took a serious blow. Two prominent employers went out of business causing us difficulty in keeping the apartments rented out. And when they were rented, the applicants didn't stay long; they were primarily moving from one place to another trying to find work. That meant we had to do whatever we could to stay afloat. Sometimes Glenn's family was the only one paying rent. Hunt got a job repairing wheel chairs for a charitable agency and I began submitting application for employment as a secretary. I had more than adequate job experience especially in church offices, so I decided to start looking. Armed with my credentials and a glowing recommendation from my last employer, West End Baptist Church, I scanned the help-wanted section of the newspaper.

A local Southern Baptist Church had an opening for secretary. I applied and was interviewed. They told me that they had received a call from Lincoln Bingham who told them of my expertise. I thought I had a good chance of obtaining employment with them, and was disappointed when I didn't get it. After thinking about it awhile, I decided to ask why I didn't get the position. A trustee told me that I should have gotten the job and would have, if I wasn't black. So that door was closed and another one opened. I was hired by Buena Vista Baptist Church (a much larger SBC) as a secretary to the minister of music- a job that fit me even better.

Nikeiva was about two months old when Glenn came home from an assignment in South Korea to see his little baby girl for the first time. His next orders were to report to Fort Campbell, Kentucky. He shared with me that he was tired of leaving his family behind so that on his next assignment he wanted them to go with him if they could. We had a long talk about his anxiety resulting from an upcoming assignment to the Sinai Desert. This concerned me because it wasn't like Glenn with his gung ho personality. I knew he needed to be bathed in prayer so I solicited others to pray with me. I told them I didn't know what I was to pray about except that it involved my son, Glenn.

I was at work on December 12, 1985 when I heard the news. "Some 248 101st Airborne Division (Air Assault) and Fort Campbell Soldiers were killed in an early morning plane crash at Gander (Newfoundland) International Airport today, returning from six months of peacekeeping duty on the Sinai Peninsula in the Middle East." The pilot and crew of eight was among the lives lost bringing total number of dead to 256. No survivors.

My heart literally broke in two as I cried, "O Lord, Glenn was on that plane! He must have felt something was going to happen. That's why he was so uptight about going." But while my co-workers were trying to console me, my phone rang and it was Glenn's voice on the other line. He was crying and said, "I'm safe and on my way home right now." How can I describe that kind of mood swing? I can't. Neither could I understand how he survived when the report said there were no survivors. His roadie and best friend perished that day leaving a wife and four children behind. Although the exact cause of the crash has not been determined, officials ruled out sabotage and the accident remains under investigation almost 37 years later. The investigation has engendered a considerable amount of speculation and debate.

The local news reporters had already gotten the scoop before I did. *Messenger-Inquirer* reporters came to our home the following day to interview us. Everybody gathered in the living room. Looking at all the thankful faces, I secretly pondered these thoughts. Was it a miracle that Glenn survived? As they interviewed him, the story unfolded. The facts disclosed that he was not on the plane because he had already gotten orders to go Germany. His superior officers let him leave two days earlier in order to process out and pack up his family. This time they would go with him. The lesson I learned from this experience was that it was not a miracle but it definitely was God's providential care that spared his life.

129

Over the years, I promised to remind him that his life was spared for a divine reason...don't waste it. By the way, Glenn knows the name of the soldier who took his place on that plane. Isn't that an awesome reminder of Jesus taking our place on the cross? Praise God!

A few weeks later, Glenn and his family got on yet another plane heading for Germany, but they were not going to be alone. Delphia and her husband were stationed there making a total of six family members overseas at the same time. Of course, losing the Davis family's rent affected our income. Like all parents, we wanted to shield Joy and Neil from the blunt of our everyday struggles with finances. Nonetheless, it wasn't long before Joy found out how bad finances had deteriorated. She writes:

CUPBOARD EMPTY

By the fall of my 8th grade year, my dad had stepped down as pastor of the chapel. We were attending a predominantly white Southern Baptist church in town. The congregants were friendly and welcoming and we felt at home there. I'd made a couple of friends at church. Christmas was coming and there was the usual excitement in the air. We busied ourselves with the usual preparations – singing Christmas carols, preparing for Christmas plays and concerts, decorating the house, buying presents. But less than a week before Christmas, Mama was admitted to the hospital with chest pains. Because of her age and race, they put Mama into the ICU. I was scared at first, but she reassured me that they were only taking precautionary measures. I cooked dinner for the family in Mama's absence and went about with my usual *chores. One afternoon, the doorbell rang and members of our church delivered a basket of food. I thought to myself, "This is one of those baskets they give to poor families. They must be giving it to us because Mama in is the hospital. That's sweet!" When I went to put the food away, that's when I realized that there was nothing in our cupboards. "**We** were the poor family!"*

We had to figure out a way to generate revenue. One of the pastors in town let us use a plot of his land to create a garden. We really grew closer as a unit while digging, planting, and gathering its produce. Remember, Hunt was the only one of us that had been reared in the country. Joy, Neil, and I were ignorant, but willing students. One day as we were planting, Hunt told me to dig a hole and put three cucumber seeds in each hole. He went on to do other sowing. After about one-half hour, he yelled over to me, "What are you doing?" I said, "Sowing the cucumber seeds as you told me to." He replied, "How many holes have you dug?" I said, "Fifty." Then he yelled, "Stop!" I had planted three seeds in fifty holes. Hunt said, "Do you realize that we'll have cucumbers running out of our noses." And we did, because once again I goofed and failed to thin them out. We got a kick out of seeing 150 cucumbers plants surviving and yielding enough to feed the entire city.

Joy and Neil saw a great opportunity to make extra money...they'd put up a stand and sell them to people passing by. Their business endeavor was a complete flop because gardens were popular in town. So, we did the next best thing...we fed the pigs with all the cucumbers we could not eat or pickle.

In addition to gardening, we started a paper route. You might recall that our family had a thriving enterprise earlier with the *Louisville Times*. Now we'd be working for the

Messenger-Inquirer. It would certainly be a challenge, but we desperately needed funds to keep afloat. Hunt had a route by himself while Joy and Neil had two together with me as their driver. This was our arrangement Monday through Saturday but we all delivered papers together on Sundays. We would wake up about 3:00 a.m., fold papers and enclose them in plastic, deliver them, and return home for about two hours of sleep before starting our day. On weekdays, Hunt and I would then go to work; Joy and Neil would go to school.

The folks at Temple Baptist Church were wonderful but we really began to miss our home church in Louisville. So we made a unanimous decision to go to West End each week for worship after delivering Sunday's papers. Our schedule had to change a bit; we had to go to bed early on Saturdays and arise even earlier on Sundays. Looking back over that time, it was hard but it was truly a blessing in disguise. This is how I see it now. When Hunt and I got married our five children all worked alongside of us. It proved to be just what we needed to bond as a unit and just what the kids needed to learn that life is all about struggling. After the struggle, growth and faith in God, themselves and others, we vowed not to change our pattern of hard work and discipline when it came to our youngest set. It was this growth and maturity I witnessed occurring again in our last two children and said, "Thank you, Lord, for the struggle."

At this point we knew big decisions had to be made. We couldn't possibly keep up this pace. It was decided we would leave Owensboro and move back to Louisville. Taking everything into account, we only had one option—chapter seven bankruptcy which meant losing the apartment building. With little income and much debt, we were thankful for the government bankruptcy option. In this manner, we had a chance to start over and get back on our feet. We reviewed the events that got us to this place. It definitely was not where we ever thought we'd be. However, it was what it was and we needed to move forward. Our application for bankruptcy didn't take long to approve; therefore, in a few weeks we packed up to return home to family and friends in Louisville leaving many fond and not-so-fond memories behind. For the next seven years, we watched every penny spent and used what we earned wisely. The bankruptcy prevented us from purchasing anything on credit. All of our troubles paled in the light of joyful reunion with loved ones. And yes, we were homeless and had to find someone to temporarily take us in until we could find a place to live. My dear mother's reminder of God's Word rang out loudly in my mind. She would say, "Cast your bread upon the waters and after many days you will see them again." (Ecclesiastes 11:1) Mama taught us to do good without expecting a reward and God would return it ten-fold.

One of the regular guests for weekly Sunday dinners was a summer missionary from Mississippi, Lillian Moore. She had completed her degree at Southern Baptist Seminary, married a military officer, and was now living in Louisville with two children. They heard of our plight and opened their home to us. Hunt had to have gall bladder surgery and it so happened that the timing was perfect. The surgery was to be performed at Fort Knox Army Hospital at the same time we were to vacate the property. So…Hunt went to the hospital to be admitted for surgery while the kids and I moved to Louisville with our belongings. We secured storage units for our home furnishings and took only minimum items as needed.

Summer months of 1988 were spent at the Mitchells' home while Hunt recuperated from surgery. Now the business at hand was finding a place to rent and enrolling Joy and Neil in Louisville public school. We found a nice house on Carnation Drive in the Pleasure Ridge Park section of town. Both children were initially enrolled at Pleasure Ridge Park

High School—the same school Del and Rodney had been forced bussed to a few years back. They didn't attend too long though. After a few weeks there, Joy felt it wasn't the "right fit" for her and applied to duPont Manual High School to take advantage of the many opportunities to excel that were offered there, such as YPAS (Youth Performing Arts Program) and the High School University program. Neil stayed at Pleasure Ridge a year before transferring to Male High, a traditional – rival school. That pleased them since they were definitely rivals at home.

I used to think surely that they hated each other the way they argued all of time, disagreeing on the smallest matters. My older children assured me that they were doing a harmless "sibling thing." There were never any serious blows given…mainly hits and quarrels. I could always look back at an incident when they were younger growing up and be assured they loved each other. One of their cousins had hit Neil and Joy attacked her with fury I had never witnessed from her before. After I broke the fight up I asked Joy, "What happened? You and Neil are always into it. Why are you defending him now?" In a very emotional voice, she answered, "He's my meat! He's my meat!" That settled it--she could hit him but nobody else could.

As expected, Joy received a full scholarship to Washington University in St. Louis and graduated with a dual degree in History and African & African American Studies. Nothing newsworthy about her achievements, since she was a straight-A student. Like the occasion when she enrolled at her new school in Louisville, the Principal looked over her transcript and asked, "Have you ever made a B?" To which she replied, "I did once." After completing her studies at Washington University, Joy went on to receive a master's degree from UAB (University of Alabama Birmingham.) Being a history major, her goal was, and still is, to study law.

But Neil's scholastic climb took quite different path. While living in Owensboro, Neil was not doing so well in school. It didn't concern him a bit that Joy was making all A's and he was making D's. I thought the reason for most of his inattentiveness resulted from the friends he kept. Now we were back home where I knew he wanted to be and it was time for a little reminder—plate breaking event was right around the corner. The two of us had a long fruitful conversation regarding what he wanted to do to prepare him to be a productive citizen. I hoped that talk would propel him to try harder. Neil excelled in English and other literary subjects but simply hated mathematics causing his grade point average to be a low 2.5.

Returning home seemed to reignite an interest in his studies. I stood amazed as he raised his GPA to a 3.5 within the subsequent years. Male High School had an Army ROTC program that was one of the most successful ones in the state; however, it was the U. S. Navy BOOST program (Broadening Opportunities for Officer Selection Training) that caught his interest. Nevertheless, he had to be accepted based on his SAT scores, grades, and etc. and he met all specified requirements. Neil left for San Diego, California right after completing high school at age 17 for extensive academic preparation. He was the first of his siblings to be away from home for the traditional plate breaking ritual.

After successfully completed the BOOST program, Neil was awarded a four-year scholarship to any college in the United States of his choice that had a Navy ROTC and to eventually be commissioned as an officer. Norfolk State University was his choice. He said he chose Norfolk because he had always attended mostly white schools and wanted to go to a primarily black college. The same student who didn't like math and avoided anything other than intermediate studies, made extra money tutoring calculus after completing the navy program and is currently seventh-grade math teacher.

Reflectively, everything was moving along smoothly for the two of us. Hunt was now approaching sixty-two and looking forward to drawing his social security which would set us up pretty good financially as an addition to his army retirement check. I guess I should has seen the next step coming, but I was truly blindsided. During a conversation after dinner one evening, he laid out his desires for retirement. It went something like this. "Honey," he said, "I've been thinking of our moving some place warm when I turn sixty-two." I said, "You have? Where?" He replied very calmly, "Alabama." I yelled at him, "Alabama! I haven't lost anything in Alabama!" The conversation that had started calmly immediately turned loud and heated disorient. I ended our talk with, "I am not moving to Alabama." Then Hunt countering with, "Then I'll go alone."

I knew the reason he "chose" Alabama. His younger brother, Alonzo, lived in Enterprise, Alabama near Fort Rucker; he had recently retired from twenty plus years in the military service. Hunt had told me that Alonzo was only three when he enlisted and could remember the pride in his eyes every time he came home on leave. Now his little brother had asked him to consider moving south to be close to him. Even though this was a wonderful reason, I definitely wasn't buying it.

I loved living in Louisville and had a perfect position at West End Baptist Church as Minister of Music with oodles of close friends. My mother was not well at the time, but I didn't use her illness as an excuse to stay knowing she was receiving excellent care. After giving me ample time and space to reconsider, Hunt told our grown children his plans. They soon understood that I didn't intend to accompany him.

You can imagine the long faces and urgent talks that pursued from that discovery. I got plenty of "Mama, how could you?"

Then one day as I was going to work, I heard the Lord's voice speaking to my stubborn heart loudly and very clearly saying, "What are you doing? You prayed for this man, I gave him to you, now you want to give him back?" I said, "So true. You did give him to me and I promised it would be for keeps. I'm sorry." When I reached my destination, I called Hunt and apologized and vowed once more to go wherever he went even if it meant moving to Alabama.

Shortly after Hunt's sixty-second birthday, we made the move. It was February 1992; it was hot, hot, hot! And it was still winter! On numerous occasions we had visited Alonzo and family, but I didn't know what to expect once we became residents rather than visitors. The transition from Louisville went mostly without a snag. We rented a large U-Haul truck to carry our furnishings. As we were loading up, Buckle saw that there might not be enough room for our grill and offered to take it off our hands. Hunt spoke quickly saying, "If I have to make a decision on which one to take, it'll be the grill; you can keep your sister." We all had a good laugh at that smart remark, but knew not to take it seriously. Hunt was known for his "flip lip" and subtle sense of humor.

Rodney and I followed Hunt the in U-Haul southward to Ozark, Alabama. We only encountered one risky incident on our move. It began raining as we came across the Tennessee hills; the truck Hunt was driving hydroplaned and all Rodney and I could do was watch and pray while it coasted into a rest area space for 18-wheeler drivers where he could come to a safe stop. We felt God's providential protection over us as we regrouped and continued our drive. After a very long commute, we finally reached our new home on Sunny Acres Drive. It was nothing to brag about, just a plain frame three bedroom house in a nice neighborhood. However, it came as no surprise that the first visitor from home was my big brother, Buckle. Once more, he took on the job as investigator coming to check out our living conditions, and I knew the reason why.

Kentucky was in the south but not in what most people called the "Deep South." There were many made-up tales along with real events that would cause any Black person to be leery of residing in Alabama. Even though it was 1992, we knew from our experiences in Kentucky that racism was alive and well. Additionally, movies seemed to always show houses in Alabama on stilts or cinder blocks with dogs and cats running beneath the house. So, Buckle came (as he put it) to check things out for himself. We chuckled privately. Hunt told me that he knew my older siblings had spoiled me rotten, but of course I wouldn't admit it even though I knew it was true. I simply brushed it off as evidence that they loved me. The look on Buckle's eyes was priceless as his eyes popped open when he saw the nice place we called home and left Ozark, Alabama satisfied that I'd be okay.

Citizens of Ozark were both friendly and welcoming which made our transition go more smoothly. First order of business for us was to check for a place to worship. We didn't care whether the church was affiliated with the Southern Baptist or the National Baptist Convention since we had worshipped with both. We simply wanted to abide by our covenant which read "as soon as you left one church you'd unite with another." The first Sunday in town, we visited Greater Sardis Baptist Church, a Black congregation, and decided we would return the next week. On our third visit we joined the fellowship and began to become active members. The congregants were friendly and welcoming; so was the pastor, at first. Hunt would be asked to fill the pulpit when he was absent. Nevertheless, he made it very clear to the pastor that he was not interested in pastoring again. But the pastor still saw Hunt as a threat and began telling his congregation not listen to any other preacher but him. Our stay there was short...less than two years.

It seemed that the same spirit existed in most of the black churches we attended, so we attempted to try out the White churches. But when inquiring about membership, at one of these churches, the pastor said, "he would guide us to a good black church." It wasn't until a friend told us about the chapel services at Fort Rucker that we knew we'd finally found a comfortable place of worship. Hunt got plenty of opportunities to teach Sunday School and other religious education ventures, while I found my place in the music ministry. Soon I obtained a government contract as music director; the pay was more than sufficient. Many wonderful things have happened since we began worshipping at Rucker, but the most endearing was getting a "new" grandson.

The Sims family attended the same chapel that we attended. Doris and David parented three sons: Adrian, Winston, and David Jr. (D, J.). Doris and I were especially close; she was like a daughter to me. Neither of us was aware that Little D. J. had been checking us out until he entered kindergarten. His maternal and paternal grandparents were all deceased and he had no one to invite on Grandparent's Day at his school. After getting permission from his mother, D. J. drew up an "adoption contract". Doris said that he wrote it all by himself on his first grade tablet with a fat pencil. He was dead serious about this adoption and so were we, never missing anything he participated in from soccer to school band. Grandparents' Day would slip our minds and the minds of our natural grandchildren, but not D.J.; he always remembered with a card or gift. I'm very proud to call him "grandson".

Joy and Neil came home for summer break each year. They loved the warm weather of L.A. (lower Alabama), the close proximity of Panama City beach, the bustling city of Atlanta, and Disney World in Orlando didn't hurt either. Neil shared this account of very special season in his life that helped solidify his appreciation for family.

TRAVELING MERCIES

Neil writes…

I was looking for a car during the summer of 1993 between my freshman and sophomore college years. One day my father suggested that we work on the old grey Pontiac that had been the family car. However, there was one slight problem, the car needed a new engine. I say slight because my father was a master mechanic. My father, my brother Glen and I spent long hours in the garage pulling out the old motor and replacing it with a remanufactured engine. Dad taught me so much that summer about cars. My brother Glenn built a speaker box. To this day, whenever I watch car shows on TV, I still think back to those happy times in the family garage working and trading stories. At the end of the summer, it was time for me to head back to college but the car was not quite ready, I was disappointed but also grateful that I had so much quality time to spend with my family and impressed that we were able to make so much progress.

Soon I was back at school, busy with my full load of classes, my part time job and Naval ROTC responsibilities and classes. During Thanksgiving break, I traveled from Norfolk, VA to my hometown of Louisville, KY. Dad and I had worked out a plan for me to pick up the car in Louisville and drive it to Norfolk for the last few weeks of class. The route back to the East Coast took me through the Appalachian Mountain chain and the transmission did not survive the trip. Everything seemed fine at first, but the changes in elevation made the transmission smoke. I had broken down nearly 300 miles away from my destination.

Stranded near Charlottesville, Virginia my only recourse was to call my family. After reaching a pay phone I spoke to my oldest sister, Debbie. She told my father and my brother, Rodney, about my breakdown. At the time, I was very disappointed that all of the time, energy and money that went into getting the car working was seemingly wasted. Nevertheless, classes were about to resume and I needed to get back, so I bought a bus ticket to Norfolk and traveled back to college.

I thought that all of our work on the car was for naught. My father and brother said that they "would take care of the Pontiac." I figured that the car would be scrapped and that would be the end of this story. To my surprise, Dad and Rodney teamed up to fix the car. They drove to Charlottesville, paid for a replacement transmission and stayed in town until the car was ready to be driven to Norfolk. I told my college friends about all that we had gone through this summer to get the car running. So when my father and Rodney showed up on campus with the car, I had no words to express my gratitude for their sacrifice on my behalf.

Years later, when I tell people this story, they are amazed and it makes me appreciate how blessed I am to be born into such a loving family.

Joy and Neil would both soon meet their potential life's mates, fall deeply in love, and marry. And just like the first five, their completion from school and their marriages would be close together—one year apart. Joy met her husband while studying at UAB and while he was serving in the military; Neil met his wife at Norfolk University where they were both students. Joy and James married in 1996 with Hunt proudly walking her down the aisle. Also in 1996, Neil was commissioned as a naval officer and a year later married Consuela with Hunt performing the ceremony. Consuela acquired her medical degree in Pediatrics. Now, we really had an empty nest. The last two had flown the coop and were soaring like eagles. What else better could any parent desire? However, unbeknownst to us, a few years later 9/11 would occur and Neil would be right in the thick of it. Here's a paper I wrote as I reflected back on that momentous event.

9/11

September 11, 2001. We all remember that day as vividly and clearly as if it were yesterday. I can safely say that most people can readily recall that day, what they were doing when they heard the news, and how that tragic event affected them. I won't go into the details, because we all know them. We were asked to 'dust off our memory caps' and share, so here it goes.

It began as a normal Tuesday morning for me. I was heading to my regular meeting at Fort Rucker to join with my PWOC (Protestant Women of the Chapel) group for Bible study when I first heard the news of the first crash on the North tower of the World Trade Center in Manhattan. While I was gathering myself, word came over our local Faith Radio Station that a second plane had crashed into the South Tower. Before I arrived at the Chapel, reports of yet another plane had crashed into the Pentagon in Arlington, VA. We soon found out later that a fourth attack was avoided due to the heroic actions on passengers and crew who gave their lives to protect our government buildings in Washington, DC. All of this devastation happened within a couple of hours. It was definitely a coordinated terroristic attack executed to cripple our nation and a personal attack on our pride. Nearly 3,000 people lost their lives on that fateful day.

Three members of my family were known to be in the direct path of the destruction, but as it turned out only one of them was in immediate danger. James, my son-in-law, lived in Brooklyn, NY but worked in Manhattan. His job sometimes caused him to go into both towers, but that day he said that he had decided to take a day off from work. He told us that he had no real reason to do so, it was just a feeling. Then there was Keith, my great-nephew, who worked for a large restaurant in New York. He was scheduled to go to the South Tower and pick up catering items that were used the night before. He was instructed to be there before 9:00 a.m. on Tuesday morning. However, someone in the Tower had called his company and told them not to be in any hurry because they had put them away in a storage closet for now.

Meanwhile, my youngest son, Neil, was serving as a Lieutenant in the United States Navy and was assigned to the Pentagon Annex. I, along with the rest of the family, was very proud of his accomplishments. Four hours crept by slowly as we awaited news of his fate. The waiting was tortuous; it seemed like forever. There was virtually no means of communication available. All transportation was halted. Consuela, his young wife, tried her best to get closer to where he was but to no avail. All anyone could do was wait and pray. Finally, we got word that he was safe and unharmed. It turned out that he was not in the Pentagon at the time of the attack; he was across the street from it in the Annex.

Neil called me later that evening and through his tears shared this testimony: "Mom, I was in the Annex building and

143

was preparing to take a completed report to my superior officer in the Pentagon. About 0900 I rose from my chair, walked over to a desk, and proceeded to lift the stack of papers from it when I heard very clearly the Lord's voice saying, 'You don't have to do that just now. Wait 'til later'. I put the papers down and within five minutes I heard a very low-flying plane come over the Annex where I was and went right through the exact door I was to go through." As he talked, he was weeping while I was both crying and rejoicing. Crying with him for all the friends he'd lost that day, but rejoicing that his life was spared.

No, we will never forget! General Ted Olson, whose wife, Barbara Olson, died aboard American Airlines flight 77, which hit the Pentagon said in an emotional ceremony, "September 11 is far more than a day that will live in infamy, as President Roosevelt said about December 7, 1941. It was a cataclysm that reshaped almost everything about our lives, the way we perceive our country, the world, our values, our liberties, our security, our seeming invincibility within our borders, and our fellow man."

Hunt helped his brother, Alonzo, with his thriving lawn care service grooming lawns of banks, post office, and other local businesses in addition those of some private home. One day while landscaping for a local bank, they were approached by a lady needing help with her lawn. The home was located in a very quiet and well-kept neighborhood. A lake ran behind it that was hidden from view by pine trees and other brush. Their job was to clear the property about halfway down to the water. conversation between Alonzo and his employee it was revealed that her home was in Chicago and the house was being restored was owned by her fiancé. She was living there long enough for the remodeling to be finished. She was looking for a good family to be caretakers when she went back to Chicago and asked him if he knew anybody that would be a good tenant.

Hunt was standing close by and told her that we might be interested. That evening we came over to look at the house and immediately loved it. We took residence of the Cherry Lane property just about the same time our lease was ending on Sunny Acres...perfect timing and what a blessing. The yellow brick house was practically new with aluminum siding, newly installed berber carpet, modern appliances plus affordable rental. Hunt and his brother planted 60 small Leland pine trees around the property down to the lake - thirty on each side outlying the grounds which would eventually provide a private fence. Our rent as caretakers remained a low $300 a month until the trees reached their maturity. Another one of God's blessings.

Nevertheless, I still missed my family and friends back home and needed to find a way to fill my lonely hours. I enjoyed restoring old furniture and found solace in buying small wooden desks and chairs from Goodwill, refinishing them, and re-gifting them back to the store. This was a satisfying way to keep me content while making someone less fortunate happy. My frequent visits to the Goodwill store opened up an opportunity for employment. I began working at Goodwill and was enjoying my part-time position when yet another job became available-substitute teaching, which was what I really desired to do. Most of my substituting teaching was done at Carroll High School because I preferred to work with that age group. I liked to think I could tell them to act their age and they would do so.

I STILL BELIEVE IN MIRACLES

Whenever I was called to substitute, my only request of the classroom teacher was that they not plan a video on the days I worked. I desired them to "give" students something they knew was of value, such as, notes for test preparation, etc. One teacher did just what I requested. Her class was generally an unruly, mix of students that were assigned to her class because they had serious behavioral problems. This teacher chose me every time she had to be out and I wondered, "Why me?" She told me that her class always asked for me. I'm still puzzled with that explanation. Anyway, this particular day I had planned out every minute of the class period allowing five minutes for roll call and closing...all 50 minutes. Their assignment was to copy the study questions off of an overhead projector for Monday's test. I gave them explicit instructions. I said, "Remove a sheet of paper, secure a sharpened pencil, and be ready to copy your study questions from the projector. There are thirty sentences on each transparency. I am allowing you ten minutes to copy ten sentences with two minutes grace time each. I will not give anyone the original study sheet. If you don't complete your copying in the allotted time, you will have get it later from one of your classmates.

After calling out orders to begin, I noticed that one girl was sitting there doing nothing while other students were hurriedly writing. I removed the first sheet and placed the second one on top of the machine when she asked, "Give me the sheet so I can copy it." I said, "No way. You've missed your chance and will miss the second group of ten if you don't get with it." Nothing more had to be said.

I loved it! Each student had his head down writing as fast as he could. I had taken a seat in the back of the room *when laughter broke out. Startled at the commotion, I proceeded to ask for an explanation. They were having a ball laughing and pointing toward the overhead projector. That's when I noticed the light had gone out and the screen was blank. I thought, "Oh no. Just when things had gone so smoothly." I walked to the front of the classroom like I had every confidence that all was under control. Next (I believe this was God inspired) I reminded them that I was a believer and I believed in miracles. I then gently laid my hands on the projector screen and wham! The light came back on. Needless to say, every student got busy writing and never looked at me the same way after that day. I dismissed class with one minute to spare.*

In my early sixties, I found time or made time for writing short stories that sparked my quest to write a book. I didn't limit myself to writing narrative; I found a new way to (should I say, express myself) through prose and rap. Yes, I said rap. When this new genre of "music" became popular in the late seventies, I though the world was literally coming to an end. Neil and I went round and round on the topic. He said rap was music and/or art. I described it as noise, plain and simple, adding that it wouldn't last long. Wrong. Rap, or sometimes referred to as Hip Hop, has now been popular field of music for nearly forty years. Because of its popularity, I knew I couldn't stop it, so I decided to join it. The picture below is of me dressed in the outfit I wore while performing.

Babbie Mason, a well-known Christian singer, wrote a song entitled, "Stay up on the Wall." It wasn't written for people to dance to, but when I heard the strong drum beat of her sound track, I felt this would be a great avenue to not sing, but speak prose to a rap beat. Therefore, the emergence of a new star was born. I took on the personae of Tina Turner, a famous singer and recording artist, right down to her fishnet stockings. By taking advantage of any opportunity that became available, I became very popular ocally. Here's something I wrote and dressed up as Tina performing in rap style for the 90th birthday party of my sister, Donzella. I was almost 71 at the time.

CELEBRATING 90 YEARS

Life is so funny
And if the truth was told;
When I was young
You seemed so very old.

But as I matured
Seems like you just stood still;

I'll never figure out that math
Cause now, we're both over the hill.

Remember, I grew up with your kids
You were just like a mother;
You had no problem correcting your young 'uns
And I got whipped along with the others.

You're soft spoken and tender hearted
To that we'd all confess;
But we have learned from experience
Not to come by you with a bunch of mess.

You're like that locomotive
That eases down the track;
You'd better move when it's approaching
Or prepare yourself for a whack.

If I were to try to list all your fine points
As I reflect over your life;
What stands out above all else
Is the extent of your sacrifice.

Others, Lord, others
Has been your battle cry;
Visiting, caring, helping the sick
May be the best kept secret for longevity yet.

So keep on doing the Lord's good work
And do it with a smile,
And you'll leave us all spinning in the dirt
As you go those extra miles.

The following years of our retirement gave us several opportunities to travel and travel, we did. I was so thankful that Hunt and I both loved to do the same thing. It wasn't unusual for one of us to suggest taking an unplanned trip to visit whomever. We both had flexible schedules so it afforded us the chance to go on a minutes notice, so to speak. I was joking with my son, Keith, and said, "We have so many children that we could just go stay with each of them for two months at a time and then start over the next year." He evidently took me more seriously than I intended, because shortly afterwards he asked when we were coming. It wasn't feasible to travel for a year, but we could visit all of them, stay. a few days with each of the married ones, and shorter time with the others.

We planned an itinerary and took off. It was October and Neil's birthday was approaching so we started with him. We traveled east to pick up interstate 95 to Norfolk and stayed in the Navy Lodge there for two days visiting Neil. Then we drove across West Virginia into Kentucky and stopped at Rodney and Diane's home in Hopkinsville, Kentucky and they stayed in their home for three days. Leaving Hoptown, as the locals called it, we went to Louisville where both Debby and Keith lived. We split a week's duration between them before returning southward toward home.

Joy was at UAB living in a small apartment completing her master's. All hotels in Birmingham were full due to the annual Magic City Classic football game which continues today as the oldest rivalry between Alabama A & M and Alabama State University. It ranks in importance for the African American colleges to that of the Iron Bowl...Alabama vs. Auburn. The closest room available was in Clanton, Alabama which is 39 miles north of Montgomery. So, we loved up on Joy all day and topped our visit off enjoying a fine dinner with her before checking into our hotel room in Clanton. We were almost through with our family excursion.

Del and granddaughter Alyssa were next on the list. We arrived in Montgomery and found our way to Maxwell Air Force Base where Del served as music director at the chapel.. After enjoying an awesome worship service, we went to her apartment in Montgomery and enjoyed a delicious meal she had prepared before heading home to Ozark. I was about to turn toward our house when Hunt asked, "Where are you going? "Home," I answered. To which he replied, "We haven't visited them all yet." I said, "What? He explained, "We said we were going to visit all of our children. We haven't seen Glenn and his family yet." Even though Glenn lived only five miles away, he said he wouldn't feel right if we left him out. So, we stopped by briefly to see Glenn, Gerrie and the grandchildren, then home sweet home after fourteen days and many, many miles.

My seventieth birthday was right around the corner and I so wanted it to be a momentous occasion. First of all, this birthday marked thirty-two years of living after surviving what could have been a life-ending occurrence. I celebrated every year after that incident happened, but my seventieth year was special for yet another reason. Psalm 90:10a reads: "The years of our life are seventy, or even by reason of strength eighty," (ESV) So reaching that landmark was very significant to me, Especially since I didn't have any major health problems and was feeling at the top of my game. My oldest sibling, Donzella, was thriving at the age of eighty-nine; therefore, I believed I had a few more good years left to live. Having a large sit-down dinner party was the first item on my agenda. I had an awesome family and an equally fantastic group of sons-in-law daughters-in-law (I like to refer to them as "in-loves"). All I had to do was share my wish with Gerrie and it took off from there.

As expected, our children instructed me to secure a venue, choose a menu, and invite friends, etc. I chose the Holiday Inn in Enterprise, and a full- course meal for $10 a person. And yes, I made a guest list, but I think my family was just a little surprised when I gave them to total guests invited...100 and counting. The party was great! Eighty-nine friends and family members came to help me celebrate. Our seven children entertained them with music and an enactment of the "breaking my favorite lamp" episode. When it came time for my closing remarks, I revealed a previously private plan to enroll in college in the fall. It came as a shock to everybody except my husband. I proceeded to share that my desire for a college education spanned more than fifty years. Getting a college degree had always alluded me. All of my children and my husband had at least an associate's bachelor's degree and I wanted to try to obtain one, too. I further admitted that I was aware of how expensive a four-year college education would be and had done some research. Troy State University Dothan (as called in 2002) offered qualifying seniors 65 years and older opportunity to get their bachelor's degree by means of a Lifelong Learning Program. A qualifying applicant would be enrolled as a full-time student with paid tuition provided as long as grades were kept above 2.0 GPA (grade point average). The party lasted awhile longer while I received many words of encouragement.

Hunt and I walked, hand-in hand, into the admissions office as I inquired into the program and after completing a simple entrance exam, it was official...I was accepted and would be the oldest student on campus. I will never forget the pride I felt as I departed Troy University that day and Hunt's motivating words. He held my hand tightly and said, "Honey, I'm so proud of you."

So many things were new to me, but my children had equipped me with a book bag on wheels, a new phone (a little more modern than a flip phone), some financial help in updating my wardrobe and plus a new computer. My first days on campus were exciting. Everybody was so welcoming and friendly. I don't exactly know what I expected, but was pleased that I didn't stand out like a sore thumb. However, I was surely behind times with the onslaught of electronic items. Case in point…walking by *the friendly students*, I nodded my head while saying "hello." I did this day after day, thrilled that everybody was so friendly before I realized that they were not speaking to me; they were talking into their blue tooth devices and most likely didn't even notice me. However, I considered it as a learning experience from which I could benefit. I would set out to prove to them and to myself that I was not on campus as a fluke.

During my freshman year, I began to get the attention of faculty by achieving outstanding grades in all of my subjects, thereby receiving placement on the Dean's and President's list many times. I had several young fellow classmates ask me how I was able to make A's in class and on exams. They seemed a little surprised when I told them that I took notes, read assigned material, and studied. The first year, I looked forward to reviewing for exams with my husband's assistance. I would type test questions out with black ink along with test answers in red ink. Each evening we would sit together while he read the question and I'd reply while he checked for accuracy. One year later things changed. Hunt began to be very confused in determining between the black-inked questions and the red-inked answers. So much so that our studying together was fruitless. I truly missed the delightful time with Hunt while he was able to fully communicate, but I knew that period has passed.

Hunt was a huge baseball fan and he knew the names of players two generations back, whereas my favorite sport was football. Nevertheless, we worked out a compromise that

153

suited us to a tee. He taught me all about baseball, such as which team is declared the winner after 7 1/2 endings along with other intricate insights while I instructed him in the rules of football. My suspicions were confirmed in 2003. The Atlanta Braves were leading by one point in the eighth inning when the umpire called the game. Hunt went on to bed after waiting for the game to continue. I stayed up until its completion. The following morn, he asked, "Who won the game?" I answered, "The Braves. It was called in the eighth inning due to rain." He said, "Where did you get that idea?" And vehemently argued, although incorrectly, saying, "That whenever there was no winner declared, the game would have to be replayed. You must be thinking about softball." All I could do was stare at him in disbelief. It might have sounded like an insignificant uttering, but hearing it flow from his lips was paramount. My husband knew the rules of baseball backwards and forwards. Something was definitely wrong, but my hands would be tied until he realized he needed help.

Months later, Hunt came to me and said, "I need help. I can't seem to remember anything these days." I made an appointment with Dr. Kesserwani, a neurologist, who diagnosed Hunt with Alzheimer's disease in October 2003. Alzheimer's is a disease that progressively destroys the memory and can adversely affect behavior, eventually leads to loss of speech and death. I would soon discover it was like a window that keeps closing a little bit more every day. Nobody could stop it.

Family members and friends did all they could do to assist me, however, I accepted that I had to bear most of the load of his care by myself. It wasn't truly a burden being confident that if the tables were reversed, he would do the identical thing for me. Most days came and went without anything humorous occurring, but I must tell you about this one instance.

Debbie, using her occupational therapy training, devised a chart to be used to prompt him to remember simple chores assigned for to him to do. On the chart was a picture of a mail box which he came to associate the drawing with retrieving the daily mail. There was also a reminder on the chart that it was trash pick-up day—Monday. Hunt became unable to remember when to do certain chores without prodding. So when Monday came around, I reminded him saying, "Honey, it is Monday. Take out the trash." He dutifully arose from his chair and went straight out to the area where we kept the garbage can.

After a while, I began wondering what was taking him so long. I went out to check on him and could hardly hold back my laughter when I saw what had happened. There he stood reaching as far as he could trying to get the last few pieces of trash from the bottom of the can. I immediately knew what he was doing, but I still asked, "Hunt, what are you doing?" He indignantly explained his actions, "You told me to take out the trash. That's what I'm doing." Case rested. He had taken my instructions literally. And he was moving the trash out of the can and placing it neatly on the ground beside the can. It was times like this that kept me going. Between being a full-time college student and seeing after me husband, I never knew what was coming next. Local Alzheimer's support groups helped me maneuver through meeting his daily needs successfully.

I surpassed my wildest expectations as a seventy-year old student. Yes, I never would have enrolled if I felt I could not retain the material, but I was surprised at how much I had remembered from my seventh grade algebra class. All I can say is to God be the glory. The Bible tells us that we are fearfully and wonderfully made (Psalm139). I repeatedly got a first-hand view of the magnificent brain God had designed and placed in this old head. In addition to commendations from

155

school officials, I was featured in local newspaper articles and interviewed on television. It seemed that everyone wanted to know how I was able to keep up my grades so well, especially doing so while caring for a husband with Alzheimer's disease.

Among my accomplishments were induction into two academic honor societies: The Gamma Beta Phi and the Alpha Kappa Delta; nominated for The Rosa Parks Woman of Courage Award, and the College of Arts and Sciences Outstanding Student Award in Social Science. My accomplishments were echoed by Delphia in the following letter she wrote to Tom Joyner, a popular radio host nominating me as a recipient for a $1,000.00 award.

NOMINATION LETTER

Dear Tom Joyner,

*My name is Delphia Macon and I would like to nominate my mother, Sue Hunt, as you Thursday Morning Mom. **I've been submitting my mother for consideration for over a year, and I won't give up until she is selected.** My mom is pure love, strength, and determination! I am #4 of her 7 children. Her first 5 children she raised alone. When she and my father divorced in the early 60's, my mom, determined to keep us together, worked two and three jobs to take care of us. She never put herself before us. Our home was a safe house in our neighborhood. Our home was (and still is) a safe haven for everyone. She's been like that her whole life—adopting anyone that she meets. Our friends all call her mom and their children see her as grandma. She ensured that we got all we needed growing up. She made sure we went to school and did our work. When they took corporal punishment out of the schools, she took notes to the school and told them that we could still get tapped! We are all grown now. Not one* *of us has been in any trouble with the law. We're all are working in our chosen careers.*

Now it's her turn and she's taken it on with a vengeance. Her one desire was to get a college degree. My mom is 74 now and graduated Dec. 17, 2006 magna cum laude from Troy University in Dothan, Alabama majoring in Social Science with a minor in English. Mom was in the top 10% of her class with a GPA of 3.89! She graduated alongside her granddaughter, Nikieva. We are all so proud of our mother. She's doing all this while taking care of my stepfather who has Alzheimer's disease and fighting prostate cancer. She also helped my brother with his children and grandchild while my sister-in-law served a one-year tour in Iraq. She's the music worship leader for her chapel service at Fort Rucker, Alabama. She helps students prepare for the High School exit, ACT, and SAT, exams. My mother is a tireless worker who gives from every part of her being. She graduated this year on Dec. 17th. Oh, what a celebration we had. If chosen for the Thursday Morning Mom I would like her to take a break and just do something for herself! She can see the fulfillment of 1 out of 3 of her life-long dreams. Goal #2—She wants to be a motivational speaker. Her first opportunity will be on MLK Day in Ozark, AL. Never in her wildest dreams, growing up in the 40's, did Mom think she would be speaking on the Courthouse steps in the Deep South. Goal #3—She plans to publish a book by the time she is 80. This award would be a much needed bonus and would mean the world to her. My mother is one of the most remarkable people I know. I'm 47 now and when I grow up I want to be just like her!

> *Respectfully yours,*
> *Delphia Macon*

And yes, I did win the $1,000 award. It was fun hearing Tom Joyner and team discuss Delphia's letter about me on national radio stations. Comedian J. Anthony Brown jokingly said, "Of course, she made good grades in history; she lived through it!" And yes, I proudly graduated from Troy University at Dothan, *magna cum laude* at the age of 74.

Meanwhile, Hunt and I grabbed every chance available to get away to visit family. It was quite amusing to hear how Hunt explained his illness. When asked how he was doing, he'd say in a somewhat braggadocios manner, "I've got Alzheimer's but it's in the early stages." Medication slowed the progression of the disease a lot; however, little by little I could feel him slipping farther away. Traveling by automobile became more and more confusing to him. On long trips, we would take turns driving, then retiring for the night before continuing the next morning. I knew that our driving to see our children had come to an end when he became argumentative about the direction while I drove. This caused me to be apprehensive whenever he drove. Hunt, being military trained and a "country boy, was taught to follow the sun for direction. Now with the progression of this terrible disease, he became adamant, insisting I was not going east. It didn't help when I showed him the highway sign was reading I-84 East. So after that trip, we turned to air travel for our mode of transportation or to only driving short distances that I could handle alone. Looming in the near future was compliance with his doctor's order to give up driving all together. I knew this feat would be disheartening and difficult; it certainly would be for me. Though I definitely understood his objection, the time had come when it was necessary to be done for safety reasons. After sweating over how to convince him to comply, I simply hid the keys and pretended that I hadn't seen them. He soon forgot he even had car keys and thankfully never asked again.

On one occasion as I was trying to help him change his disposable underwear, he unexpectedly slapped me very hard and told me to leave him alone. I knew he wouldn't have hit me like that in a thousand years, but I also knew it was time for me to seriously consider placing him in a long-time facility. The State of Alabama had three Veterans nursing homes that were available, but only two were within a reasonable distance from Ozark. After visiting Bill Nichols State Veterans Home in Alexander City, I made my choice. It provided 24 hour nursing coverage, a physician on call 24 hours, and on site physical, occupational and speech therapy with pharmacy services available. Upon closely observing the staff's interaction with patients (and doing the smell test), I made application for his stay. I was told there was approximately a six month waiting list which turned out to be very accurate.

An admission supervisor had to come to Ozark to observe his behavior and environment first hand. She explained that it was important that the applicant was not combative. They had to very selective regarding admission of those who are because of their military past. I convinced her that Hunt was not an aggressive person, in fact accept for that one occasion, he was extremely peaceable and cooperative.

Nonetheless, when I received notification that he was eligible for admission, my heart sank. Yet I knew that this move would be best for both of us. I packed up the clothing and other personal items he could take with him. It was February 24, 2009. Our great-grandson, Isaiah, was born on the night before taking Hunt to Nichols and a grandson, J.P., was marking his ninth birthday. It just showed me that life is like this...change happens and we must learn to adjust accordingly and go on. And it goes without saying that our children were supportive as usual.

Delphia and Joy went with me to Bill Nichols for support. Even though I knew it was for the best, it was hard leaving him there. The Bill Nichols Home was about a 2 ½ hour drive from our home in Ozark. I started out making the trip weekly, but soon found out that I couldn't keep up that pace, so I began visiting him every two weeks. Several friends traveled those miles back and forth with me.

Hunt was still able to walk alone and carry on spotty conversation with others at the time of his admission to Nichols. The Alzheimer's patients were kept on the fourth floor of the facility. The patients who were mobile wore alarm bracelets on their ankles to prevent them from leaving the area. I was kept abreast of some of the harmless antics in which he participated. His roommate was a retired night watchman so every night he would get up around 2:00 a.m., fully dress himself and walk the hallways of the fourth floor. I learned that he had a helper in Hunt who would get up, dress himself and walk the halls with him.

There are so many memories I wish I had space to share, but let's just say that I will always hold them close to my heart. A poem written by an unknown author entitled, "Reason, Season, Lifetime" expresses my first encounter with Levelma Simmons. The poem states that "people come into our lives for a reason, a season, or lifetime." When someone comes into your life for a reason, it is usually to meet a need you have expressed. Lee's husband was a resident at Bill Nichols the same time Hunt was there. A mutual acquaintance introduced us and she immediately gave me a bank stub with her telephone on it. Then she quipped, "You are welcome to stay in my home when you need to come for an early appointment here. I live alone in a big house and would love to have you stay. And if you want to deposit a little something into my bank account, you have all the information at hand." I knew right off that she was a friend for a reason that I'd want around for a lifetime.

Making trips to Bill Nichols every two weeks was a huge challenge to place on my 1998 Toyota, Rav 4, but she held up really well given that her mileage gauge increased by more than 38,000 miles during Hunt's time there. On January 7, 2015, I was notified that Hunt's death was imminent. I notified all of my family members, pastor and everybody else I could, soliciting their prayers. The next day, January 8th, he quietly slipped away into the hands of Jesus with me by his beside along with Pastor Breckenridge, Glenn, and Levelma. We prayed and sang hymns. It was definitely the most beautiful worship experience I had ever witnessed. Finally, I was led to whisper these words into his ears, "Hunt, you will never know how many times I've thanked God for sending you into my life. You were just what I needed, but now it's your time. Go. Jesus is waiting for you. Rest assured that I will be all right and will join you in heaven." As my words ended, he took his last breath. Hunt's death came just four days shy of his 85th birthday, January 12th. His remains were returned home to Ozark with home-going service held at Fort Rucker Main Post Chapel on January 17, 2015. It was definitely a celebration with many memorable moments that included our children and grandchildren singing a favorite song of his— *Total Praise*. After full military rites, his body was laid to rest at Woodlawn Memory Gardens.

My desire to write and publish a book before I reached eighty years of age was put on hold over and over again until now. First, it was having to finish college which was challenging in itself; then adding Hunt's illness and care, I hands my hands full. Now, after his death, I had free time to write. I was 83 years old and without excuse, but the procrastination continued even after receiving encouraging words from all venues—family, friends, and members of the McGee Writer's Forum to which I belonged. In my defense I can say they were obstacles of a good sort. It appeared that every time I'd get ready to write, something else would pop up that needed my attention. One such occasion was the deteriorating condition of my beloved's final resting place…Woodlawn Memory Gardens. What I saw occurring there nearly six months after his burial shocked me into action. I wrote following article for our local newspaper, *The Southern Star*, for publication.

WHAT IS HAPPENING TO WOODLAWN MEMORY GARDENS?

In the eyes of this observant… not much of anything right.

Twenty-four year ago, my late husband and I moved to this area to retire. We were attracted to Ozark because of its small-town appeal and friendly residents along with the fringe benefit of being close to Fort Rucker. We loved it then; I still love it now. It is because of that love that I hate seeing this beautiful place in desperate need of repair and maintenance.

In 2001 we made a decision to permanently make this our final resting place by entering into contract with Woodlawn and securing burial plots. Since my husband was retired military, there were monetary advantages to be had by doing so. Under said contract, we agreed to abide by the rules and regulations set out by the Trustees of Woodlawn Memory Gardens. In return Woodlawn agree to provide several specific services, such as, "perpetually cause the grass on said property to be maintained at reasonable intervals and in addition keep in repair and maintain in good condition all buildings, drives, lawns, trees, and borders in the said Woodlawn Memory Gardens of Ozark."

As you can readily see in the photos taken on May 9, 2016, Woodlawn has not held up their part of the contract.

In addition to broken up interior roads, others concerns have come to light. Here is what I want readers to know.

- *Woodlawn Memory Gardens is not listed in the Ozark telephone book making it virtually impossible to reach staff for their services.*
- *They are located in Dothan; the Ozark office is unoccupied; therefore, personnel are only there by appointment. (Nothing is posted on the door to indicate such, for example, a telephone number or name of a contact person)*
- *I have talked to several people who have loved ones buried at Woodlawn. They complained of unsightly grass and weeds around the markers and sunken graves. Another person told me that his mother passed away and was buried in Woodlawn in March 2015 and after over a year her date of death was still not on her marker.*
- *These are gross conditions. The walkways and drives cannot be fixed by pouring a little concrete in them as they have done recently. The only doable solution is for Woodlawn to black top roads with asphalt.*

Dear Reader, I have tried to communicate to you as much as I know. Many of you that are in the same predicament as I am. I challenge you to speak up. Let's do this to honor our loved ones. Together we can see Woodlawn restored to the beautiful, serene place that we can be proud to make our final resting place.

By Sue A. Hunt

May 28, 2016

Before writing the article of May 28th in the *Southern Star,* I appeared before our Ozark City Council and laid out area residents' complaint against the Glenco Services of Dothan who held a 2016 Ozark city license to operate. The Council was very receptive to me and voted to write a letter to Glenco on our behalf. The letter they sent was both thorough and forceful. Additionally, the City Council pointed out their disgust concerning the ragged condition of the American Flag onlookers witnessed being attempted to be raised during the annual Memorial Day Observation. An ultimatum was given to Glenco to respond to the Council with plans as to how they would resolve these issues by July 1, 2016. Glenco made no attempt to respond. So I preceded in another direction. I placed a second article in the Star. This time it was to galvanize citizens into action thus causing them to become excited about remedying Woodlawn's poor conditions. And it worked.

My next move was to call a meeting of anyone who had a complaint against Woodlawn. Several people expressed their outrage over the non-response from Glenco Services. Thirty-one outraged residents showed up at Ozark Dale County Public Library for the assembly, during which time we documented a number of diverse complaints, such as date of death not on deceased grave markers, sunken graves, and the inability to reach personnel. I discovered that the Alabama State Department of Insurance, Preneed Division handled all such complaints involving grave sites and I came to the gathering with the proper forms. Anyone who had grievances of this type would have to submit a formal complaint on a form entitled, "Consumer Request for Assistance".

I am proud to say that our combined efforts were successful and the majority of our demands were met. (Inner roads were patched not black topped). However, on the positive side, the Ozark office now has a full time employee, groundkeepers are cutting grass and weed eating in a timely fashion, date of death on headstones and markers are installed. Oh yes, the ragged American flag has been replaced.

My involvement in the improvement project ingratiated me with community leaders and renewed my interest in civic affairs.

PART IV

MOVING FORWARD

So, there you have it. As promised, I have told you the story of me and you can see that I was not that special by a long shot—only in God's sight. Longevity appeared to be the norm in our family. Most lived past the age of seventy. My mother died when she was 102 years of age and my father lived nearly 73 years. My oldest sibling, Donzella, recently passed away at 103 years of age; my oldest brother, Frank died at the age of 71 years, while my twin siblings lived long lives, too—Maxie lived to see age of 87 and Howard (Buckle) died at age of 91. Ruben Lee (Pete) died at the young age of 55 years, while Julia Mae passed away at 68 years. Yes, God has blessed us with many fruitful years on the earth and I am grateful.

Now at 85 years of age, I am often asked what I see my next step being. My answer--I don't know. However, I do know I will stay busy and involved as long as my health allows. I love to write so I'll most likely remain active in a writers' groups of some kind. And of course, I will continue to do all I can for the advancement of Christ is kingdom locally and abroad. How could I not? I credit all of the achievements I've had so far in my life to the Lord. Yes, I, like any believer, had to undergo times of testing to toughen my spiritual muscles and endurance while He taught me to rely on Him. I am still a work in progress…still attempting every day to be more like Christ. As you read my story about my ups and downs, it is my deepest desire that you see and understand the bigger picture. We are not perfect; we all sin; we all fall, but what matters most is what we do when we get up. My sentiments are best expressed in the lyrics of a well-known gospel song by Andrae' Crouch entitled, "Through it All."

I've had many tears and sorrows,
I've had questions for tomorrow,
There's been time I didn't know right from wrong.
But in every situation,
God gave me blessed consolation,
That my trials come to only make me strong.

I've been to lots of places,
I've seen a lot of faces,
There's been times I felt so all alone.
But in my lonely hours,
Yes, in those precious lonely hours,
Jesus lets me know that I was His own.

Through it all, through it all,
I've learned to trust in Jesus, I've learned to trust in God
Through it all, through it all,
I've learned to depend upon His Word.
The End

INSPIRATIONS

Additional Writings
Prompt: "At the very moment she realized that the only thing left to do was to pack her car and hit the road." Written after Delphia totaled her car, Betsy Mae.

OBITUARY
2002 -2016

Little Miss Betsy Mae departed this life on Friday, July 8, 2016 in Birmingham, Alabama at the age of fourteen with a total of 500,342 miles. She was the adopted by Delphia Macon in 2004 when she was only two years old. Her natural parents decided to discard her after accumulating what they thought to be a disability due to her high mileage of 40,000. (Toyota has never built a better model, according to Delphia, than the 2002 4-runner).

Some of Delphia's best memories with Betsy was their alone time. After seeing the movie *War Room,* she wanted to set up a prayer room but didn't know where that place should be. Realizing that she spent so much time with Betsy, Delphia set up her war room right on the steering wheel!

Betsy's service record was outstanding. She traveled countless miles over the United States and repeatedly voyaged to her hometown of Louisville, Kentucky. Many admirers witnessed seeing her going throughout numerous counties in Alabama, thereby benefiting her loving owner financially.

Most importantly, this brave servant risked her life to protect Delphia from serious injuries as well as the other driver involved. Betsy came out scarred and bangled, but not even that ordeal stopped her heart from beating. Delphia testified that when the wreckage company pulled her into her final resting place, they started her engine and she purred softly like a kitten.

Delphia's family extends her gratitude for all who prayed for her during this difficult time. One friend wrote: "My condolences for your loss Delphia. It is appointed unto cars once to die, then the judgment. When Betsy Mae sees the Mechanic in the sky, hopefully he will say to her 'well done my good and faithful vehicle!' that is, if she was converted. Only those filled with synthetic oil are his."

On this coming Sunday, Delphia will adopt yet another Toyota 4-runner. This time it will be a 2001 that has under 250,000 miles on it. Her name will be Hattie Jean. It is her prayer that Hattie will be as faithful as Betsy. But for now she has to leave Betsy behind and go forth. *At that moment she realized her only option was to remove her belonging from Betsy and hit the road driving a Chevy Cruze rental car.*

Hard Times

Prompt: "Write a paper using only one syllable words." This is a story my mother told me when I was quite young.

Hard Times

Sue Hunt   2-18-16

My Mom told me of a time when both funds and food were low. There was not a thing in the ice box to eat, and not a thing left on the shelves but flour. Her spouse had drunk up all the dough so there was zilch to make a meal for her six kids the next dawn. Of course, she was vexed but not like one with no hope. This place led her to do what she had done time and time o'er...pray.

Near dawn, Mom heard a faint knock on the front door. It was Miss White. She had come down from the big house with a large bag crammed with scraps of ham and fat back. Her Spouse had told her to throw it out in the slop, but she knew Mom could use it. Since her mate was not wild about black folk, he would just throw the good meat out in the trash. My Mom would tell us the Miss White had a good heart: a heart full of love for all. Mom thanked her for her gift and then thanked God for His day in and day out care.

She took the port fat, cooked the oil out of it, and made hot bread with the flour she had. Next, she cooked the ham and topped it off with red sauce from the dregs left in the pan. A strong smell flowed through the whole house and soon there were six small mouths gung ho to eat. They all dug in and yelled, "Mom, this is the best meal of all."

NOTE: Here are two truths one can take from this tale: God is an on time God and He has no hands to use but ours.

Whose Rib Am I?

Delphia wrote *"Whose Rib am I?"* while stationed at Eglin Air Force Base, 1985.

Whose Rib Am I?

It is not good that man should be alone,
I will make him a help meet fit for him...

So the Lord caused a deep sleep to fall
upon the man, and while he slept took
one of his ribs and closed up its place
with flesh; and the rib which the Lord
God had taken from the man He made into
a woman.

"This is, at last, bone of my bone and flesh
of my flesh. She shall be called woman
because she was taken out of man!"

Am I a woman? I am. Then whose rib am I?
Women ask themselves and wonder every day:
whose rib am I? It's a baffling question,
isn't it? Yet, a lot of women go through life
not knowing whose rib they're made of. So
many unhappy lives are lived because the
answer to the question is not known.

Whose rib am I?

Some man is walking around without a rib
because I was made. Someday he will find me,
and he will be my true love. And that day
he will ask me, "Whose rib are you? And
I will say, "I am yours."

ENDORSEMENTS

In telling her story, Sue Hunt has spoken the language of every wife, every mother, every daughter, every sister, and every woman friend. In the valleys and the mountain top experiences the underlying themes are interwoven in the fabric of family and togetherness and sewn with the strong threads of love.

Sylvia Malone

Sue Hunt's life story is one of overcoming, faith and most of all, love. Her strength is unveiled as she tells the events of her childhood, early marriage, raising of her children, and finally finding and losing the love of her life. Her story is nothing short of remarkable. I am honored and blessed to know Sue Hunt and to call her 'friend'. You will be blessed, and inspired, to read "Mary the Last".

Helen Taylor Andrews

I met Sue Hunt when my family and I first attended Headquarters Chapel at Fort Rucker, Alabama, in the summer of 2014. Her first question to me was, "Do you sing?" I answered, "Yes, but not well." Her follow-up was, "Would you sing a solo for us in the service next week?" How could I refuse? Even though the government contract which paid Sue to serve the congregation was later discontinued, she has joyfully continued to serve, to the great benefit everyone. In fact, she has served the Fort Rucker Army community in numerous ways, earning her the Volunteer of the Year Award for service to the entire base. She has been a wonderful encouragement to me, my family, and many others. We will not, on this side of Heaven, know the true reach of this one humble servant of God. It is an honor to call her "Mama."

Chaplain (Major) James P. Breckenridge, US Army

PHOTOS:

"Who am I, Lord God, and what is my house, that You have brought me thus far?   (2 Samuels 7:18)

Mama with daughters:

Sue, Donzella, Mama, Julia, Maxie

Names on picture of Mama and sons:
Buckle, Pete, Mama, Frank

My seven children in chronological order:

Neil, Joy, Rodney, Del, Glenn, Keith, Debby

My grand and great-grandchildren:

Back roll – Markesse, Nicholas, Ronnie, Bryan, J.P. holding Maya

2nd Roll— Nikeiva holding Desmond, Tiffany, Aly, Lakeisha, Avory

1st roll –Rodney, Edward, Isaiah, Zayla, (Me), Zion, Nia, Ian, Chara

- Missing from photo: Jackie, Christian, Ava, Ebony, Damone, Brentyn, Derek, Olivia, D.J.

83668042R00099

Made in the USA
Lexington, KY
15 March 2018